Praise for *Generation X Presidents Leading Community Colleges*

"This book provides an insightful narrative of the motivation, experiences, rewards, and styles of today's Generation X community college leaders. Stable, effective, and courageous leadership is critical to the success of our colleges and to their capacity to meet the needs of today's students. The authors present a refreshing perspective on changing leadership competencies, the importance of 'fit,' the value of mentoring, and how to bring balance to the all-consuming life of today's community college leader."

—**George Boggs**, PhD, president and CEO emeritus, American Association of Community Colleges; president emeritus, Palomar College

"The contributors to the book explain how leaders in the Baby Boomer generation have held the reins in many colleges, leading Generation X workers in day-to-day activities. However, scores of the Boomer generation are now exiting the workforce, leaving the leadership reins in the hands of Generation Xers. In doing so, though, they'll not only be leading their fellow Gen-Xers and the younger Millennial workers, but they'll also be leading Baby Boomers and possibly some older workers from the veteran generation who are still in the workplace. What does this mean for community colleges? This book shows that this generation of leaders represents a leadership transition the likes of which the sector has never seen before, due to the stark differences in values between the two dominant generations. This twelve-chapter book opens with an introduction to the new challenges facing presidents and then progresses with discussions on the generational differences; leading from the middle; becoming and remaining a president; intrusive mentoring; new strategic planning; and final chapters focusing on contemporary aspects of Generation X leadership. The chapters are composed of several defining parts that maintain a sense of continuity throughout the book. An overall value of this book is that it reminds the reader that higher education and society in general are changing, so it's only natural that the next generation's leadership style will change as well. Gen-Xers are different; they're working in a different era and they have different values and experiences that they bring to the table. In other words, this book forwards the reader to expect Gen-Xers to bring a different style of leadership to the institution. This book can be an excellent resource for emerging leaders, senior leaders, faculty, boards of trustees, and the leadership enthusiast."

—**Christine Johnson McPhail**, president, McPhail Group LLC; leadership coach, Achieving the Dream, Inc.; faculty, Roueche Graduate Center; men   College Advisory Board

D1562557

"The changing landscape of America's community colleges requires a different type of leader, one who is able to tackle emerging challenges such as developing multi-cultural communities that foster inquiry and action; reforming developmental education in a way that is connected with a program of study; moving their colleges to the center of their communities; and using technology to improve teaching and learning, rather than as an end to itself. This study of Generation X presidents is critical at time; the nation is depending on their leadership to take community colleges into the next wave of innovation and difference making."

—**Karen A. Stout**, president and CEO, Achieving the Dream, Inc.

Generation X Presidents Leading Community Colleges

Generation X Presidents Leading Community Colleges

New Challenges, New Leaders

Edited by
Martha M. Ellis and Linda L. García

AMERICAN
ASSOCIATION OF
COMMUNITY
COLLEGES

ROWMAN & LITTLEFIELD
Lanham • Boulder • New York • London

Published by Rowman & Littlefield
A wholly owned subsidiary of The Rowman & Littlefield Publishing Group, Inc.
4501 Forbes Boulevard, Suite 200, Lanham, Maryland 20706
www.rowman.com

Unit A, Whitacre Mews, 26-34 Stannary Street, London SE11 4AB

British Library Cataloguing in Publication Information Available.

Library of Congress Cataloging-in-Publication Data Available

ISBN: 978-1-4758-3152-8 (cloth : alk. paper)
ISBN: 978-1-4758-3153-5 (pbk. : alk. paper)
ISBN: 978-1-4758-3154-2 (electronic)

♾™ The paper used in this publication meets the minimum requirements of American
National Standard for Information Sciences—Permanence of Paper for Printed Library
Materials, ANSI/NISO Z39.48-1992.

Printed in the United States of America.

For the past and current community college presidents who paved the way; the aspiring community college presidents who believe in changing student lives; and the mentors who said "just do it."

We especially thank our families, who continue to support our dreams.

Contents

Foreword

More than 900 presidential transitions have occurred in the last five years in community colleges. That's not a wave of change—that's a tsunami. And it's had a domino effect on colleges, as the leaders-in-the-wings—vice presidents, deans, etc.—rise up to fill those presidential positions and create more vacancies.

Colleges are scrambling not only to hire replacements, but also to prepare the next generation of leaders. It's essential that, when the time comes, those that want leadership positions are prepared to take them on. Leadership training has become critical, from national programs like the American Association of Community Colleges' Future Leaders Institute to "grow-your-own" programs at the college level.

But I recognize that it's not only important to give rising leaders tools—to teach them about budgets and boards and policies—but to also let them walk their own paths. Though the community college mission has not changed, our students have. They expect a different learning experience than the students of twenty, or even ten, years ago. These students also represent diverse backgrounds and needs. Serving them, and helping them succeed, requires innovative thinking. The rationale of "this is the way we've always done it" is no longer acceptable in today's community college.

Leadership requires motivation, forward-thinking, and the nerve to take risks. The new generation of leaders will face a world that is ever-changing; from technology to politics they will have to navigate carefully as a community college president. This book is filled with advice and examples from Generation X presidents who are tackling today's challenges in order to take community colleges into the future. They are in the hot seat right now, handling an array of issues: budget crises, developmental education reform, the demand for more accountability, and the need to mentor and support their own successors, to name just a few.

The editors, Martha Ellis and Linda García, bring a wealth of knowledge on this topic. Martha has been a college president and an instructor, and has facilitated AACC leadership institutes. She's been a guide and mentor to new and future community college leaders. Linda's work at the Center for Community College Student Engagement has given her a deep understanding of what today's students need in order to succeed—something that's on the minds of all leaders.

Being a community college president is not a glamourous job, but it is immensely rewarding. To those of you who are new to the role, welcome. Much of your training will happen on the job, and this book will be a valuable resource in your toolbox.

Walter G. Bumphus, Ph.D.
President and CEO
American Association of Community Colleges
Washington, DC

Acknowledgments

A book of this nature requires the contributions of an amazing group of leaders. We acknowledge and are grateful to the nineteen Generation X presidents who took time during their demanding personal and professional schedules to share their insights on being a community college president. We are extremely appreciative of the candor and courage with which these presidents responded to our questions about themselves and community colleges. We have taken precaution to ensure the confidentiality of each president while providing results of the study. The chapters written by Generation X presidents center around topics of their choosing. We thank these authors for their time in contributing their thoughts and ideas as we seek to further understand the challenges and rewards of the community college presidency.

We are also grateful to previous generations of community college leaders who provided the foundation and mentorship for these and countless other presidents. The idea for this book arose from conversations with these leaders in concert with Generation X leaders.

No one becomes a president alone and no one writes a book alone. One needs support and encouragement, experience, and expertise to write a book. We are indebted to many people who provided these elements to make this book a reality. On the home front we thank our families and colleagues. A special thank you to Sarah Jubar, acquisitions editor, and Bethany Janka, assistant editor at Rowman & Littlefield.

Introduction

Generation X Presidents and New Challenges

Martha M. Ellis

Why can't culture and strategy have breakfast together?

—Joe Shaffer, President, Laramie Community College, Wyoming, 2015

Community colleges are facing unprecedented challenges including with a seismic exodus of successful presidents. Fortunately, a cadre of Generation X campus presidents and CEOs is taking the helm to lead community colleges through the evolving landscape. Their voices are often not heard in the literature or at conferences but they are the future of community college leadership. They are also the leaders who will be mentoring and planning for the next generation of community college leadership. This book is about them; their voices and their leadership.

At the 2015 American Association of Community Colleges (AACC) convention, there were two sequential concurrent sessions addressing the presidential role: one panel featured the legends of community colleges; the next session featured a panel with Generation X presidents. The spark was ignited as to the similarities and differences in responses by these two panels about the presidency and future of community colleges. While talking with presidential colleagues, doctoral students, and current faculty at community colleges, what motivated baby boomers to become presidents may not be motivating Generation Xers. While leaders and faculty of the younger generations love to hear the stories from the legends of the silent generation, they may not be able to relate to this discussion. Are generational differences impacting the decision of not becoming a college president? How do we encourage talented individuals to take on these important leadership positions?

THE LEADERSHIP CHALLENGE

Walter Bumphus, president and CEO of the AACC, reports that over nine hundred presidential transitions have occurred in the last five years. Bumphus went on to say, "Although we have tracked this data for five years, no one could have predicted the tsunami of leadership transitions in community colleges" (Smith 2016). One of the great demands facing community colleges today is lack of talented and skillful presidents. Leadership matters. Upon reviewing the research from Achieving the Dream, Aspen Institute, Community College Research Center, the League for Innovation and other organizations working in the community college space at the national level, competent senior leaders are identified as vital to meet the challenges of today's community colleges.

The flood of imminent retirements of sitting presidents and other senior leaders from community colleges is widely known. It is estimated that 43 percent to 50 percent of the presidents will retire in the next five years (Lipka 2013; Wyner 2014). O'Banion reports that 75 percent of the presidents have announced plans to retire in the next ten years (Smith 2016). Boggs reports that "leadership turnover rates will continue to be high at a time when strong and stable leadership is needed" (2014–2015).

What is often overlooked is the number of presidents choosing to leave the presidency earlier in life for another career. The League for Innovation 2015 *Trends Report* (de los Santos and Milliron 2016) relates the modal presidential tenure is one to five years compared with six to ten years in 2007 and eleven to fifteen years in 1997. Cook (2012) reported the average tenure for a departing CEO was eight and a half years in 2006 compared to seven years in 2011. In California, the average length for a college president and chancellor is only 3.5 years (Cooper 2016). A shorter leadership life cycle may be brewing for presidents. As one Generation X president reported:

I have been a president for 10 years and I am in my late 40s. I do not see myself doing this in 10 more years.

Commitment is important to Gen Xers. That commitment is to the mission and idea of community colleges, rather than a particular institution. The commonly held belief by this generation is that they are responsible for their future. There is no expectation that the college will be there for them in the future. As long as the culture of the community and college mesh with the values of the Gen X president, they are highly committed to that institution. However, when situations change, these presidents may choose to move on. One president explained how the culture of change is impacting the length of staying in the presidency.

Community college culture is changing, causing presidents to move around or leave totally. We must help presidents stay in positions longer. What can we help teach them about warnings and ways to get through the tough times?

Another president talked of the tendency of presidents to move too quickly when times get difficult.

Some of my colleagues move too soon. I believe it is best to hang in there for the long haul. Sometimes presidents jump when things get messy. I firmly believe in dealing with conflict and staying committed to the college and the community.

The need for skillful community college presidents is not new. The seminal work *Shared Vision: Transformational Leadership in American Community Colleges* (Roueche, Baker, and Rose 1989) was a landmark study identifying the skills that were required to meet the challenges of the 1990s and beyond. The authors recognized community colleges were facing new challenges. Skillful and transformational leaders were critical for community colleges to succeed in a changing landscape. Men and women were needed with the ability to influence and motivate faculty and staff to work with them to transform the leader's concept of what the future should be to accomplish the mission of the college—a shared vision.

Are these skills the same for today and the third decade of the twenty-first century for community college leaders? Yes, but additional skills will be needed. "Meeting new expectations will require a new vision of leadership. The skills and qualities that made community colleges' presidents effective when the dominant benchmark of success was access alone are no longer the same now that expectations extend to higher levels of completion, quality, and productivity" (Aspen Institute and Achieving the Dream 2013, 2).

Simply stated by a Gen X president:

There is not anything new under the sun. Even when older colleagues were new to the job, they tried things that had not been tried before. There was a lot of entrepreneurial spirit in the past. The idea might be the same but the context is different. When the older generation started, they were not operating with the technology, social media or concept of global competition that forms the backdrop for Gen X leaders.

Leaders from younger generations are needed who understand new priorities, feel the urgency to focus, and are ready and willing to make hard decisions was one of the major findings in the *2015 Trends Report* (de los Santos and Milliron 2016). As two presidents articulated:

We do understand why it is different today. Hard decisions need to be made. We all need to acknowledge the context is different from previous generations.

Being an effective community college president is a difficult job with arduous job requirements; especially with the increasing emphasis being put on outcomes, accountability, and equity, internal pressures from other administrators and faculty, and external pressures from state government(s) and the community being served.

Wyner (2014) reports for award-winning community colleges, where change has taken hold, the presidents have an average tenure at the college of over ten years. Generation X presidents have difficulty with this timeline.

Taking ten years to bring about change and make an impact does not resonate with Gen X presidents.

I have a different level of urgency with the evolving mission of community colleges. I feel a sense of urgency to get it right quickly.

The changing landscape of community colleges has generated a multitude of questions and anxieties. There is concern that talented younger people are consciously choosing not to seek the presidency. The seemingly daunting challenges facing executive leaders of community colleges can paint a negative picture. As one Generation X president stated:

There is so much negativity: budget shortfalls, politics, colleges being pawns, faculty not happy. It is an ugly picture with little prestige. Helping people to achieve goals is hard work. We need a campaign for leadership that says the reward is worth the hassle.

Couple this with the barrage of media about the scarcity of people to fill the many presidential vacancies and there is potential for a self-fulfilling prophecy of no one wanting to become a president. A point of contention with younger presidents is remarks from leaders inside and outside of higher education that lament there are few college presidents today who are like the giants of previous generations (Selingo 2016a, b). The interviews with Generation X presidents reveal the potential for filling the perceived void with the new giants in the field.

Peter Drucker said "Culture eats strategy for breakfast." From a Gen X perspective, "Why can't culture and strategy have breakfast together?"

NEW CHALLENGES FACING COMMUNITY COLLEGES

Community colleges are undergoing significant change often referred to as "disruption," or even revolution, due to the magnitude of the proposed transformation (American Association of Community College 2012; Aspen Institute 2013; de los Santos and Milliron 2015; Tugend 2016). An in-depth discussion of the multitude of challenges currently facing community colleges is not the goal of this book. Rather an overview of the confluence of economic, demographic, learning science, and accountability changes identified by Gen X presidents provides the foundation for understanding the challenges and opportunities facing the current and future presidents.

Financial

The reduction in financial resources is a common theme heard by presidents of all generations across the country. State appropriations to community colleges have eroded. A stark example is the zero funding Maricopa and Pima Community Colleges now receive in the state of Arizona. States are increasingly tying funding to student completion metrics as the model of funding. Thirty states have moved to or are in the process of moving to performance-based funding ranging from 100 percent in Ohio to 10 percent in Texas (Quinton 2016). The unpredictability of financial resources from state coffers is requiring leaders and boards of trustees to consider increased tuition and/or increased millage, levies, or property taxes. These are not optimal solutions for students or the local community.

Partnerships are embraced as colleges alone cannot meet the needs of the community and students. This calls for integration among regional ecosystems, including K–12, colleges, universities, social service agencies, and employers. The merger of community colleges with each other or with universities is a progressively accepted option epitomizing the ultimate partnership.

And of course, there is increased pressure on presidents to become chief fundraisers. From applying for a variety of sometimes unrelated grants, spending increasingly more time with potential donors, to participating in the swelling numbers of fundraising events, community college presidents are realizing raising money for the college is a primary criteria for success.

Nearly ten years after the onset of the Great Recession, the harsh economic realities experienced by higher education show few signs of improving (Ostashevsky 2016; Selingo 2016a, b). Most leaders in and researchers of community colleges concur the "good old days" of funding are not coming back.

Our (Generation X presidents) business model is murkier, and our expectations for success and accountability are increased and broadened.

Enrollment

Even when funding is a performance-based system, enrollment will impact the bottom line. According to AACC, community colleges have seen decreasing enrollment since 2010. Part of this decline is due to lower number of high school graduates. Children under the age of 18 accounted for 36 percent of the US population at the end of the baby boom, and today they make up just 24 percent and by 2050 they will account for just 21 percent of the population (Selingo 2016a, b). Adult students who chose to come to college during the 2009 recession are now going back into the workforce due to an improved economy. The puzzlement is that in the last two years the numbers continue to decrease when these two factors have become relatively stable. What are strategies a president and leadership team can employee to increase enrollment?

Affordability

Randi Weingarten, President of the American Federation of Teachers, said, "We now believe college is as vital as high school, yet still accept that it is increasingly unaffordable and inaccessible to many Americans" (Tugend 2016). When Pell Grants started in 1976, the amount covered most college expenses. This is no longer true. Loans have become the principal way students are making attending college a reality. In 2012, 71 percent of students graduated from colleges and universities with debt averaging close to $30,000 (Carey 2015). Part of the rhetoric and alarm over student debt may be warranted but some scholars are identifying the vilification of any education debt as undermining access to higher education. College is not seen as an investment and students who can benefit most from responsible borrowing are discouraged from even attempting college (Ort 2016).

America's College Promise is one experimental approach to address affordability and keeping the open door to community colleges. Free tuition to community college students who meet qualifications is being implemented at individual colleges, in cities, and in some states. As this book is being written, the presidential campaign of 2016 is in full swing. One of the higher education platforms is free tuition at public colleges and universities. While there is a national discussion, a federal program is not likely to be enacted so the pressure is on states to examine a plan, such as Tennessee Promise (Boggs 2015). College is never free. Either donors, or students, or taxpayers, or a combination of the three pay for the education (Ort 2016).

Completion Agenda and Accountability

In addition to reduced and unpredictable funding, the increased cry for accountability (Boggs 2015) and transparency is adding pressure to community college leadership. Almost universally there is agreement that community colleges must improve student completion numbers. The growing focus on completion must not lead to restricted access for students, particularly the people traditionally disenfranchised from higher education.

Crisis and Opportunity states that "community colleges will for the foreseeable future be expected to produce more degrees of a higher quality at a lower cost per-student to an increasingly diverse population" (Aspen Institute and Achieving the Dream 2013, 2). Who can forget the billboards in Texas (2011), financed by a business council, that stated: "Austin Community Colleges has a 3.9 percent graduation rate. Is this a good use of your tax dollars?" Graduation rate is an example of current methods of measuring higher education productivity that do not capture the work of community colleges or the students who they serve (Boggs and McPhail 2016).

Colleges are developing new strategies to increase completion rates and close the achievement and skills gap of an increasingly diverse student population. Real-time data and predictive analytics to guide and tune change initiatives to optimize outcomes for diverse students are being deployed. A more accurate data framework to measure community college productivity still needs to be developed.

Time to Degree and Credit Hour Accumulation

The time to degree and excess accumulation of semester credit hours (SCH) by students on their way to degree completion, transfer, and the labor market is a concern voiced by elected officials, business leaders, and taxpayers. For example, in Texas, the average number of credit hours earned by associate degree graduates was ninety-two SCH for a sixty SCH degree taking almost five years (THECB 2016). The recent book by Bailey, Jaggers, and Jenkins (2015) *Redesigning American's Community Colleges* proposes that guided pathways for students into and through the college experience can reduce both time to degree and excess SCH accumulation. AACC Pathways Project is working with thirty colleges across the country to implement pathways at scale and research if this approach will improve student outcomes.

External stakeholders are asking for efficiency and effectiveness. Corporate leaders encourage the efficiency mantra: *faster, better, and cheaper* be applied to higher education. Community colleges are being required to increase the number of students earning a credential with labor market value in less time with reduced funding to an increasingly diverse population.

Teaching and Learning

What goes on in the classroom is the heart of the completion agenda. Research has shown that working harder with the current models of instruction is not closing achievement gaps for many students. The learning experience is hetero-geneous for students as various pedagogical models are being implemented to address the diversity of the student population in community colleges. Examples of these learning models include competency-based, hybrid, personalized, modular, and traditional classroom augmented by technology. Recognition of these new pedagogical approaches was expressed by a president.

Students expect an individualized, high-tech, interactive experience. We have to change our practices to meet a different kind of learner.

Progressively colleges are being held accountable for demonstrated attain-ment of student learning outcomes that are clearly defined and aligned for students to obtain cognitive and noncognitive skills necessary for the future workforce. Faculty are integral to the accomplishment of this work as they are the experts in their respective disciplines. How does the president provide leadership and support without mandating and destroying the delicate dance that creates the magic of learning when a student connects with that learning outcome crafted and coached by the faculty member?

Safety and Security

Safety and security are increasingly a priority for community colleges. Community colleges have not been immune to crises on campus. Shootings on campuses in Oregon and Texas are recent examples of attacks on students and employees. Community colleges have experienced these types of inci-dents for years. In talking with presidents from all generations they report on individual incidents. These incidents, however, were unusual and not part of the conversation in leadership circles.

What is different today? Boggs and McPhail 2016 posit that the "highest priority for the community college president must be the safety and well-being of students, faculty, and staff" (166).

Being ready for any crisis from hurricanes, to mass shootings, to cam-pus carry, to assaults is one of the required responsibilities of leadership. Presidents are preparing for a variety of situations with crisis management teams and simulations to test out processes should the unthinkable happen. ACCT now provides a safety summit during the annual trustees' conference. Recent examples of mishandled crises have led to the end of the tenure of otherwise successful presidents. The president is being held accountable for the safety of students, faculty, and staff. At the same time this accountability is a challenge within itself.

When information is instantaneous the president no longer controls the narrative. In the case of a shooting on campus people expect to get the information immediately and use social media to spread their own comments on the situation. If a president makes a misstep, it's assessed in all different angles (Ashford 2016).

New Leaders to Address New Challenges: A National Research Study of Generation X Presidents at US Community Colleges

Community colleges are facing new challenges as well as the extraordinary numbers of successful presidents leaving their positions. Fortunately there is a cadre of young, Generation Xers who are campus presidents and CEOs willing to tackle the demanding and complex issues facing community colleges. With that in mind a representative group of successful Generation X presidents were identified.

Methodological Foundation

Nineteen Gen X community college presidents participated in individual semi-structured telephone interviews describing their journeys to becoming a president, the presidential experience, and recommendations to boards of trustees, current stakeholders, and future leaders.

The sample was diverse:

- Ages: thirty-four to fifty years of age covering the complete range of the Generation X
- Children: fifteen of the interviewees had children under the age of eighteen
- Gender: twelve men and seven women
- Ethnicity: five Latinos, two African Americans, eleven White, and one Native American
- Geographic: twelve states represented
- Location of college: urban, suburban, and rural
- Length of time in the presidential position: one week to twelve years
- Size of college: fall 2015 enrollment seventeen hundred to twenty-eight thousand students
- Doctoral degrees: eighteen had doctoral degrees representing ten different universities
- Presidential Position: nine of the presidents are CEOs who report to a Board of Trustees, ten are campus presidents

Both researchers conducted sixteen interviews and one researcher did the additional three. Transcripts were read and summarized by each researcher. The researchers used coding techniques to examine the major open-coding categories, creating appropriate subcategories. The researchers had biweekly discussions to confirm categories and subcategories. Relationships among categories became evident and generalized conclusions were drawn.

Purpose of This Book

This study of Generation X presidents identified and described a representative group of Generation X presidents in US community colleges to obtain information on how and why they became college presidents and why they stay in the leadership position. From listening to these presidents, an understanding emerged as to how they handle the all-consuming role of the presidency. The responses to the semi-structured interviews were incredibly open and transparent. The distinct techniques they utilize in accomplishing the newly defined duties and responsibilities of the presidency came to light during the study.

Not all information gained from the presidents during the interviews was included, but all information was useful in shaping the book. Due to the candid responses to the interview questions, the researchers guaranteed confidentiality to all presidents protecting the potential for possible adverse consequences from internal and external stakeholders. Approval was received from all interviewees to use information and quotes from the semi-structured interviews. Throughout the book quotations from the interviewees are provided in italics so the reader can "hear" the voices of the presidents. Multiple quotes from multiple presidents on a topic are distinguished by "a dot" in front of the quote. Brief personal vignettes from Gen X presidents who are contributing authors are in boxes interspersed in the book.

Chapter 1 provides the definition and description of the multi-generations and how the multigenerational research applies to this study. Chapters 3, 5, and 10 are the results of the study. Chapters 2, 4, 6, 7, 8, 9, and 11 are topics discussed in depth by individual Gen X presidents. The book concludes with recommendations for presidential preparation. The first section of chapter 12 includes recommendations directed to the community college field writ large. The second section is an exploration of the top ten areas for learning when an individual is considering a presidency.

The knowledge gained from listening to the voices of these presidents will be beneficial for leading community colleges today as well as the development of future leaders. An additional goal of this study is to encourage talented Generation X and Millennial individuals to become community college presidents. Leadership matters. Community colleges need strong, courageous leaders to address the challenges and opportunities for students, local communities, and the nation.

Gen X presidents do not care what happened yesterday. We are moving forward. You have heard the expression of viewing a situation as the glass is half full or half empty. Gen Xers want to know who drank the water.

Chapter One

Who Are the Generations?

Linda L. García

I attended a large meeting with presidents and chancellors. I noticed that only a few people were probably Gen Xers. The ideas and thoughts that were shared collided between the generations.

In today's environment, there are four generations working side by side: Silent Generation, Baby Boomer Generation, Generation X, and Millennial Generation. Since these generations are known to see the world differently from one another—experienced different cultural events, established different values, motivated by different messages, and identified with different heroes—there can be challenges for these four generations working together. This is a brief description of these generations.

The *Silent Generation*—born 1928 to 1945 and also known as The Forgotten Generation—were raised by parents who survived the Great Depression (Strauss and Howe 1991). This generation worked hard to maintain job security due to their parents' experiences. Working at a single organization/company was considered an obligation, a long-term career, and the pathway to earn authority in a top-down business environment. Generations after them may view this group as great mentors, too focused on being politically correct (Lancaster and Stillman 2002).

The *Baby Boomer Generation*—born 1946 to 1964—grew up during the Vietnam War, human rights movement, and antiwar and government protests (Strauss and Howe 1991). They have been identified to be skeptical of authority. As a result of their large demographic population, the Boomers became competitive with each other especially in the work place. They feared time off would result in losing their place on the corporate team. They were often seen as having an imbalance between work and family (Lancaster and Stillman 2002). Regardless, they are known for their optimistic perspectives,

including viewing work as an adventure. Other generations may view them
as workaholics and too political.

Generation X (also known as Generation Xers)—born 1965 to 1980—is
known as the "latchkey" population for constantly being left home unsuper-
vised during their youth while parents worked (Strauss and Howe 1991). This
experience created the need to become self-reliant. Since they viewed their parents as workaholics, they focused on family and work balance and an informal
working environment that embraced flexibility. While the Silent Generation
values a hierarchical system and the Baby Boomer generation is doubtful of
authority, Generation X is known to be direct toward authoritative figures when
seeking understanding and guidance (Lancaster and Stillman 2002).

The *Millennial Generation*—born 1981 to 1986—have never known the
world without technology (Strauss and Howe 1991). In fact, technology
became their way of interacting with the world at any time and any place.
The Pew Research Center (2010, 1) state, "Steeped in digital technology
and social media, they treat their multitasking hand-held gadgets almost like
a body part." Their work ethic, not mandated to long working days, is connected to feeling a need to make a great impact in a collaborative setting.
Millennials thrive in friendly and less hierarchical organizations. They seek
balance with work, life, and community involvement. Older generations may
view Millennials as needing more focus and discipline due to their multitasking nature (Lancaster and Stillman 2002).

These generational differences continue to be highlighted throughout the
chapters. For instance, the constant balancing act between managing work and
family priorities as a community college president can be a challenge. They
acknowledge the Baby Boomer generation for increasing awareness on this
concern. However, the Generation X presidents now speak about the importance
of surrendering to the challenge and integrating both experiences such as taking
family to the college's games or work conferences and hosting events at home.

> *Baby Boomers started to influence the need to balance work and life. I find ways
> to take care of myself such as playing golf with friends, practicing on my guitar
> and being attuned to my spiritual side.*

Also, Generation X presidents discussed the value of working a flexible
schedule rather than an 8 am to 5 pm schedule which they perceive is very
important to generations before them. Generation Xers appreciate the freedom
to control their schedules, which allows for personal time such as exercising
and attending their children's school events. A Generation X president said:

> *The values are different between the generations. Millennials want to bike and
> have flexible schedules, but they work really hard. People in their 70s may be
> more scheduled rather than being flexible. Board members might want a presi-
> dent to be at every meeting face-to-face, but the younger generation is comfort-
> able with participating remotely.*

And, even though this generation is comfortable with e-mails as a main source of communication, the Generation Xers understand the importance of knowing the preferred style of communication for older and younger generations. They believe face-to-face communication or phone calls are critical for the Silent Generation and Baby Boomers while social media and blogging are appealing to the Millennial Generation. All in all, Generation Xers believe they must utilize a host of communication tools to engage various stakeholders.

The Generation Xers shared that today's challenges of community colleges are very different from the challenges experienced by previous generations.

- *The Silent and Baby Boomers were working at a time when colleges were bursting at the seams. Now, there are federal and state policies and initiatives such as access, success and completion, and accountability. We need to prepare for the current community college environment. Would the older generation understand why we (Gen Xers) lead the way we do in result of the national initiatives? Older generations didn't have those national initiatives. The older presidents are designed for the past time. But, they may not realize how to adapt to the current community college environment.*
- *The way the presidential role is introduced or talked about has to change. The presidential role of today has been redesigned with current issues and is not based on what the president role was like a long time ago. The president of today is about involving disruption for success and utilizing technology and social media.*

Additional comments regarding generation differences include the following:

- *There can be a generational gap of ideas between a president.*
- *Older generations may not understand about multitasking and technology. Technological tools are different. We are accustomed to looking at the cell phone during a meeting. The older generations may find this disrespectful. There can be some challenges between older and younger generations.*
- *We want to be more involved in the discussions on national committees. We don't want it to happen without us. There needs to be a wider representation of younger leaders in those discussions.*

The four generations—Veterans, Boomers, Xers, and Nexters-have unique work ethics, different perspective on work, distinct and preferred ways of managing and being managed, idiosyncratic styles, and unique ways of viewing such work-world issues as quality . . . just showing up for work" (Zemke, Raines, and Filipcszk 1999, 25). Table 1.1 shows the types of perspectives that each generation has for other generations as described by Zemke, Raines, and Filipcszk (1999) throughout their book.

Table 1.1 Perspectives that Each Generation Has for Other Generations

What the Other Generations Say About Them	Silent Generation	Baby Boomers	Generation X	Millennials
Silent Generation says . . .		"They talk about things they ought to keep private." "They are self-absorbed."	"They don't respect experience." "They don't follow procedures." "They don't know what hard work is."	"They have good manners." "They need to toughen up." "They're smart little critters."
Baby Boomers say . . .	"They're dictatorial." "They need to learn flexibility and adapt better to change." "They're technological dinosaurs."		"They're slackers." "They're always doing things their own way, instead of the proscribed way." "They spend too much time on the Internet and email."	"They need more discipline from their parents." "They need too much attention." "Can they do my web page for me?"
Generation X says . . .	"They're too set in their ways." "They've got all the money." "Jeez, learn how to use your email, man!"	"They're workaholics." "Lighten up; it's only a job." "They're too political, always trying to figure out just what to say . . . to whom . . . and when."		"Here we go again . . . another self-absorbed generation of spoiled brats."
Millennials say...	"They are trustworthy." "They are good leaders." "They are brave."	"They're cool. They're up to date on the music we like." "They work too much."	"Cheer up!"	

Chapter Two

Leading from the Middle Generation Position

Gen X Presidents

Thom D. Chesney

Compared to many of our business and community partners and peers, today's college president is much more likely to be responsible for comfortably and adaptively navigating as many as five generations in the workplace (Ellis 2007). At any given meeting, voices and views spanning from the Greatest Generation to the latest generation bring not only richness and diversity to the conversation, but also the potential for conflict, confusion, and misunderstanding. So, how then does a Gen X president—typically seated in the middle of this spectrum—effectively enter, lead, engage, and communicate with an institution and all its stakeholders and audiences alike?

THE SEARCH PROCESS

Part of the answer is embedded in the process through which an applicant becomes a candidate who later becomes a president. Most presidential search advertisements include a detailed profile—an institutional wish list of qualities, skills, prior experience and education, and essential characteristics of the college's next leader. It matters less whether a consulting firm or the college alone composes the profile. What matters most is that it becomes the agreed upon public statement of what the institution wants and hopes for in its president. As such, it is worth the same scrutiny and attention that you would give to the final draft of a doctoral dissertation.

Presidential profiles that focus on the previous president's achievements, a newly adopted multiyear strategic and campus master plan, or both may suggest that the governing board is more inclined to hire a president comfortable with the status quo than a change agent with a fresh set of eyes. Gen X candidates might be more drawn to and likely to attain positions at colleges looking to undertake their next phase of development and redesign or which are looking for an inclusive, unifying leader who will also bring creativity and innovation to the campus. No word says "changes" quite like "change," but it is nonetheless codified in many a profile.

The later stages of a search can be equally telling. The composition of search committees, irrespective of whether they wield little or a great deal of influence in the final selection, can also send signals about whether an institution is looking for someone to engage and include the entire spectrum of employees in undertaking initiatives that will move the college forward. Similarly, as more Gen X presidential candidates enter the market we must expect and prepare for questions that allude to or directly address the perceived qualities and traits of our generation. Consider, for example, a common question like, "What would a typical workday look like for you—when would you arrive and when would you leave?" On its face, this question leaves little room for the occasional telecommuting morning ahead of a lunch meeting with an alumnus, followed by an afternoon on campus seguing into your child's middle school basketball game before a harrowing return to campus to take in an intercollegiate version of the same. Translated, the real question might be, "Can we count on you to be here when we are and when we would like to see you, which is pretty much Monday through Thursday from 9 to 5, with the occasional exception for a reception, concert or guest speaker?"

As the majority of presidents retiring today are Baby Boomers and the number of qualified applicants who are Gen Xers continues to rise, it seems reasonable that "compare and contrast" questions like these would be asked. It is important for candidates not to be deflected but rather to seize upon them as opportunities to show their qualifications and to bridge the generational gaps in ways that build credibility and calm alike.

Take the preceding "typical workday" question as an example. A good answer for a Gen Xer might be,

I'm not sure there is any such thing as a typical workday, or for that matter a typical workweek. What I do know is that it's going to be very important for me to be both literally and perceptually present at the college and in the community. I suspect there will be many days when I may be the first person to arrive at the office, and on some of those I may return home in the afternoon for a dance recital or pep rally before coming back to the college to see a play that night.

An answer like this provides valuable information to a search committee that it might not otherwise get due to restrictions on what they can and cannot ask. In this case it reveals both the work ethic that is required of the president but also some information that personalizes the discussion and shows that the candidate has other interests, values personal time, but will every bit be as present in the job as anyone could expect.

This example also illustrates one of the common predicaments of the Generation X presidential candidates—how much personal information to reveal that is outside the typical scope of the interview process. Regardless of any search committee rules that may have been imposed, it is important to understand and accept that as a candidate for the top position of a college you are likely to be run through one or more search engines which, if you are at all active on social media, within the community, and in your current and previous positions, will reveal that you may have a private life, a significant other, one or more hobbies, and perhaps even a colorful past.

That said, as a candidate you should never assume that every search committee and forum audience member has scoured the internet for the good, the bad, and the ugly. Gen Xers are typically not shy about sharing information outside the lines of their application materials and interviews. There is an argument to be made for doing so and another for being cautious, but if you are tempted at any stage to be or appear as anything less than truthful, you should reconsider continuing in the process.

THE OFFER

But wait, there is more. At the point at which you have accepted the presidency, you also typically gain access to an abundance of additional information which could not have previously. Budgets and pending litigation are presented in greater detail; documented and undocumented policies, procedures, and practices are presented in voluminous binders or (hopefully) on a thumb drive. Because it is strongly advisable to take a month or so off for renewal and revival between your previous position and assuming the new one, it is important to request some addition information essential to a more successful presidential onboarding and transition.

One valuable resource is a fairly standard human resources report that includes all current employees by work group—faculty, staff, administration—job title, date of original hire, date of last promotion, initial salary, and current salary—preferably in an electronic spreadsheet that allows you to re-sort and recalculate fields in various configurations. It will, for example, make it immediately apparent roughly how many employees from each generation comprise the workforce.

Breakouts by work group might also show that median faculty longevity far exceeds that of staff—a potential employee retention or compensation concern. Administration and faculty may be disproportionately Baby Boomer compared to a much higher percentage of Generation X, Y, and Millennials in the staff ranks, classic conditions for potential communication challenges, and differing philosophies on work ethic, work hours, and even what constitutes work.

Although it is important not to jump to conclusions from a single report, there can be real value in utilizing and sharing your "findings" when you step into the job. If you plan to conduct a listening tour or other series of meet and greet opportunities in order to get to know your employees beyond the relatively few minutes you shared in the search process, knowing something about the generational demographics can help you create and navigate these audiences to greater return on your investment of time.

HIRING AND EVALUATING

Another key set of opportunities and challenges for the Generation X presidents to weave their leadership style into the fabric of the college is through the hiring, engagement, and evaluation of employees. Within existing policies that apply to each, there remains typically a great deal of latitude for presidential participation. In the case of hiring, for example, as vacancies within existing positions become available due to retirement, resignation, or other termination, it is not uncommon for the president to be informed and even included in the decision to refill the open job.

In the first year, these are perfect opportunities for a different set of curiosity questions such as "How do we usually decide whether to refill a position? What are the criteria? Do we budget at the same salary or a lesser one? Why?" and so on. You do not have to stop down the hiring process or become meddlesome, but you should take every opening you have to remind hiring supervisors and search committees of your expectations and their accountability. If the budget is stable, but static, and the college is looking to start new programs, grow enrollment, and improve retention, then it may not make sense to hire to the credentials and skills of a former incumbent when a position becomes open.

During a change in the strategic priorities and vision for a college, the president might (re)engage with the hiring process in a complementary manner, as well. For the first two years of my presidency I rarely participated in the employee interview process for positions that did not report to me or one of my direct reports. After the college went through the processes which one year led to defining and committing to our shared core values and the next to our new strategic plan and vision, I amended my approach and routinely asked to meet with finalists in a variety of roles—especially new or redesigned positions—solely to introduce these two key elements of who we are and to get a sense of whether candidates could see themselves as supporters and stakeholders of both. I made it clear to the hiring supervisors that the recommendation for hire and accountability thereafter remained with them, but I also wanted to ensure for candidates that a general familiarity with 'why we are here' was included with discussion about what and how they would be doing their prospective job.

Similarly, employee success and development is an avenue through which Generation X presidents can cultivate expectations and engage colleagues college-wide. You will undoubtedly learn early on such things as whether faculty and staff development are coordinated independent of each other, funded equitably, of high quality, and encouraged or required. Do not underestimate how something that may comprise a very small fraction of the operational budget may have an immense impact on both employee morale and political maneuvering.

On the topic of evaluation, depending on their pathway to the position, Generation X presidents may find themselves predisposed to favoring models of continuous feedback and improvement over the traditional annual performance review. It is fortunately possible to merge the two, especially if the latter is again a requirement of policy and procedure. It is useful here to share a few words about HR protocol across the five generations in the higher education workplace. In the span of about a month while drafting this chapter, each of the following events took place:

1. A 20+-year Baby Boomer employee scheduling an appointment through my assistant in order to offer her letter of retirement with a full semester notice so we could begin to plan for her departure.
2. A Millennial employee of less than six months submitting his two weeks' resignation by e-mail, with the primary reason that "nobody told me it would take so long to get promoted here."
3. A Gen X faculty member resigning effective immediately with two weeks remaining in the semester in order to take a job that was more challenging and aligned with his life's dream.
4. A Z Generation student worker and recent graduate informing me she hoped I would "move up from Twitter and Linkedin and at least get Snapchat" before she returned in a few years to take a job at the college.

With such a mix of expectations and communication styles like these spread across nearly a thousand full- and part-time employees, it is no longer feasible or manageable to provide one-size-fits-all performance evaluation.

Fortunately, as president you are in a position in which you can influence, ameliorate, and improve evaluation systems. By choosing to share experiences such as those listed above, with your talent development staff and cabinet, you are in a position to rethink how you go about onboarding, engaging, and evaluating employees. Millennials and the next generation of employees are much more likely to expect and accept continuous feedback—project-based, short-term/small incentives, before sending them off to their next assignment. These are the same colleagues who are comfortable and outspoken when telling me that my handwritten birthday cards with semicreative rhyming couplets "are nice, but a gift card to Chick-fil-A would be way more useful."

Gen Xer peers are more willing to forego the gift cards for more regular doses of feedback that provide enough specifics to help sustain or adjust a course but not so much that they cannot claim the outcomes as their own. Many Baby Boomers, however, would become crestfallen if the annual face-to-face review was reshaped into a recurring ten minutes at the top of a monthly one-to-ones or supplanted with standardized evaluation forms with a memorandum and running list of works-in-progress. Because evaluation is in part linked to morale, engagement, and future performance, it is important not to take it lightly and to encourage forms that meet the spirit and intent of what is required while connecting with the employees to fit their personalities and when and where they are in their career pathway.

COMMUNICATION

From the initial stages of the presidential search process, to establishing yourself in the role of president, to building the employee base that will ensure a college's vitality and sustainability, it is ultimately all about communication. The Gen X president leading from the middle of five generations must be adaptive and respectful of widely varying expectations. If transparency and information sharing are at all important to you, then figure out as many ways as you can to get the word out.

A monthly Board and College update, for example, that is disseminated college-wide via e-mail may get a very close reading by your Boomer employees but go unnoticed by Gen Xers unless you provide a lead paragraph with three bullets that summarize the whole thing. Take that a step further for Millennials and Zs by crafting an e-mail subject header that does the same but with even fewer characters; then, post a link to the entire update on your personal and college social media platforms and intranet portal, if you have one. And by all means, respond personally to those who comment on your correspondence, preferably using the same conduits they do. It shows respect and adaptability alike—vital traits for any president.

There is perhaps no better and no more complicated time to be a college president. The teaching and learning landscapes are changing almost daily. Presidents must be adept at looking and thinking inward and outward simultaneously as the decisions they make for their institutions can have significant impact on the surrounding community and vice versa. The best advice is if you can be genuine through it all, you will weather it all. And remember these words from a university chancellor almost thirty years ago: "Remember, the most important person in the room is a matter of perspective." Lead from that position and you are likely never to be left behind.

Human Resources Leadership with Multiple Generations
Thom D. Chesney

I began my presidency about two weeks before a few dozen individuals who had accepted early retirement, had their contract nonrenewed, or were terminated, completed their final day of employment with the college. A budget rescission at the state level had necessarily impacted the college, and employee morale was suffering to say the least. Hearing during my first month a litany of long-term complaints and concerns which contributed to some significant rifts among the three work groups, I invited the interim president who had also retired and was generally well respected to undertake a series of discussions with employees about the root cause of dissatisfaction pervasively present. Anonymous surveys, suggestion boxes, and interviews supplemented the work of a diverse employee panel that met monthly before presenting and submitting to me about a dozen key findings and recommendations.

Some of them were immediately actionable—expanding access and options for employee wellness programs that used college facilities, for example. Some would require policy change that would require Board review and approval, such as undertaking a comprehensive market compensation review of all employee categories and positions. All of them were—for the first time—pulled together into a single report, agreed upon and written by a representative group, and shared publicly with the entire college.

I took the latter step, having heard ample examples of panels, task forces, and other bodies undertaking special projects that had led to little or no action and a limited audience that received the final work product. I also decided to sustain permanently the panel itself, but recast it into an employee success team that would continue to assess employee morale formally and informally, provide a forum for discussion and ideation, create events and opportunities for employee engagement within and beyond the college, and continue to work on items laid out in the original report. Today this team supports a redesigned professional development center and staff that continues to create and deliver content that fits our changing workforce, varying schedules, and learning styles.

Chapter Three

Why We Became and Remain Presidents

Martha M. Ellis

Filling the many presidential vacancies in US community colleges is a challenge resonating throughout leadership circles. Community colleges face a crucial leadership crisis, and the concept of leadership has been studied, scrutinized, and analyzed for the last seventy-five years. Much is written about the components and behaviors exhibited by those who are deemed successful community college presidents. The literature and research of the community college presidency is deficient in why people choose to take on these complex, difficult, and challenging positions. Once they accept these senior leadership positions, what motivates CEOs to remain when times are good and when times are tough. Understanding the motivation and reasons Gen Xers chose to become and remain presidents provides insight into how this generation approaches the presidency.

WHY BECOME A PRESIDENT

Making a difference in students' lives and the community led the reasons for choosing to be a president. Repeatedly the presidents talked about believing community colleges are the primary institution for transformational change for individuals, communities, and our nation. Generation Xers are motivated to address the challenges of today. The opportunity to make a difference by improving and helping the community permeates their reasons for choosing this leadership role.

- *I took a non-traditional path as I came from CPA firm. I wanted to make a difference and impact the community. The motivation was different as through the presidency I saw a greater way to contribute. I wanted the*

13

college to come together and be more strategic to address the needs of our community and our nation.

• *This is an awesome time to be in higher education because of the evolution/ revolution and redesign. Our workforce is having DNA modified to match new population.*

• *I wanted to be part of a generation of leaders that will help community colleges take place in hearts and minds of America. This crosses all party lines and must be a unifying factor for a lot of people.*

• *Great leaders can help reshape the narrative of community colleges. Community colleges are the only institution that can change and impact social inequity.*

Expanded Influence and Impact

The work is too important not to do it. Excitement about the impact and influence they can bring to the college and community exudes from every conversation with these presidents. They do this because they want to make a difference. The drive is inside. It is not and cannot be for the money. All positions within a community college contribute to the success of the students and college, but being a president expands the span of influence. The position of president provides the opportunity for impact at a larger scale to create and shape the future.

• *I grew up in a small town and teachers had good jobs so I wanted to be a teacher and a coach. I seemed to be a natural at counseling so moved into school counseling and then college counseling. I moved into administration to influence and make decisions as well as have a broader level of impact.*

• *The presidency increases my span of influence. I still associate with students in the classroom. At the same time I influence employers in our community.*

• *I wanted to be more effective in changing and cultivating others by being higher up on the food chain. I also wanted to be a model for younger, Latina women.*

• *The presidency impacts so many people and is the position that can transform institutions. The position allows for the formation of a vision, guidance on problem solving, and impacting so many areas.*

If Not Me, Then Who?

The presidents wrestled with the question, "If not me, then who?" A belief in the community college mission and success for students undergirded the desire to utilize leadership skills at the community college rather than elsewhere. Observing decisions being made for the wrong reasons, alternative solutions not being mentioned, and the "wrong people" leading the political realm of higher education, these presidents felt an obligation to take on the position.

- *If not me, then who? I can do better than those old white guys. Egotistical men will always jump to these jobs and that is not what is always needed. I feel an obligation to use my leadership skills in the community college environment.*
- *I started as a counselor and saw the impact on students, especially first generation students. I then moved into planning and institutional research. Someone told me one day you are going to be a community college president. If I don't then who will?*
- *Old white men irritate me the way they were leading colleges. I wanted to help out on the issues of equity to promote economic and social justice.*
- *I wanted to move up in administration because I observed others and I wanted to do things differently.*
- *I finished my master's degree in higher education when I was 23 years old. As I moved into colleges, I observed decisions being made for the wrong reasons—sometimes for political advantage. The decisions were not being made for the best interest of students. So, I decided I needed to move into the role.*
- *From age of 12 I wanted to be a college professor. From age of 20 I was on the path to administration and becoming a president. I was in student government as an undergraduate and kept asking why do we do things the way we do it. This questioning was the basis for me moving into administration and a presidency.*

Students at the Center

The presidency helps facilitate student success. Money, position, power, and control are not the reasons the interviewees went into this position. They want to be strategic in ensuring that all students can learn. These presidents strive to make strategic decisions by questioning the current process. They want the student experience to be intentional. They felt an obligation to take on the president's role and impact students on a larger scale to make things better.

- *I am not motivated by money or power. I care about people—the students and the faculty.*
- *I was first generation college student and had a low income so this is very personal. I have a passion to see students persist and complete.*

- *I did not plan to go into administration. I was a first generation college student. I made fun of community colleges until I took a course at a community college to prepare for the university. The teaching and learning process was different from the university and I decided I wanted to work at a community college. At 20 years of age I had my first job at a community college. I had a passion for teaching and learning and wanted to be a dean or vice president as I felt I had something to contribute. Then there was leadership crisis that included a dysfunctional board. I felt if I did not become the president the only people interested in the position would be motivated by power, money and title and that was not good for the college. It is a calling and the right thing to do for the right reasons.*

A Good Fit

Finding the right presidency is critical to success. It has to be "a good fit." Choosing to be a president is dependent upon finding the right college. Saying no to a presidency that is not the best for the individual and the college, can be liberating. A presidential candidate needs to be the right person at the right time at the right institution where he/she can make the most difference. By doing due diligence, candidates are better informed about the mission, culture, values, and needs of the college while interviewing, and before accepting the job. They agreed that if a person does not share the same values as the college and the community when considering a specific presidential position, do not take it. Each leader confirmed a good fit with the current college at this point in his/her career.

- *Expectations of this presidency fit my work style, ethics, and life.*
- *You have to be at the right institution at the right time for where you are in your career.*
- *I am a campus president now. I may look at a chancellor's job one day but I am not ready now.*
- *Everyone who is a finalist in the presidential search can do the job. A person needs to decide if I am a good fit for the college as well as a good fit for me. Understand the good and the bad and then see if this position will be healthy for me and healthy for the college. I am interviewing the college as much as they are interviewing me.*

Encouragement by Others

Only three interviewees actually had the goal of becoming a college president. The remainder of the leaders explained that someone else saw the talent and abilities in them. They were tapped on the shoulder and encouraged to try on new leadership roles. Four initially resisted this encouragement saying they did not want to be a president. As they experienced more leadership roles, the desire for senior leadership role began to grow.

- *I did not want to be a president. I am a first generation college student. I got an academic scholarship and the speaker at the ceremony was the VP of student services. I decided I want to be in the field of student affairs. I started at a university but moved to community college because of the mission of the college. I worked in student affairs and became a vice president. I thought that position was where I would stay for the rest of my career. My president put the bug in my ear. I did not hear her at first. When a presidency came open several people encouraged me to apply for a presidency. The path of student services is not the usual pathway to the presidency but others encouraged me to take the chance and I am glad I did.*
- *People believed in me and encouraged me. Becoming a college campus president became a goal.*
- *I did not initially want to be a president. Other people saw a presidency in me before I saw it in myself. I wanted a meaningful life and wanted to make a difference. I had to find out if I could translate my values of creating a meaningful life in harmony with the functions of the presidency.*
- *I stumbled into community colleges. I was encouraged to step into the presidency. I have a tenacious appetite to solve problems.*

The encouragement the leaders received might have been years or a few months before they applied for their first presidency. The timeline for becoming a president varied and for three the opportunity came about when least expected.

- *I had encouragement early in my career. I accepted any opportunity that came along and had various roles and continued to receive encouragement. I did get discouraged when older sitting presidents would say to me "you never want to do that as a president or that was not presidential." About 6 to 7 years ago, I decided it was time to try it on and to articulate differently.*
- *As a student I was involved in campus life. Got interested in student success. I saw change in students and knew I wanted to make a difference and do something I love. I got my doctorate with the goal of being a university professor. I would go to conferences and the banter was negative rather than trying to make things better. A mentor suggested I explore community colleges. I spent a day with a community college president and I knew this is what I wanted to do if I had the opportunity.I did not initially want to be a president. Other people saw a presidency in me before I saw it in myself. I wanted a meaningful life and wanted to make a difference. I had to find*

out if I could translate my values of creating a meaningful life in harmony
with the functions of the presidency. That opportunity came along much
more quickly than anticipated.

WHY REMAIN A PRESIDENT

These successful Gen X presidents are motivated and enthusiastic about leading community colleges in the twenty-first century. They are articulate and
realistic about their characterization of the role and function of the community college president. Gen Xers admit they are skeptical but think this might
be beneficial for the leadership roles today.

Much attention is given to the many complex challenges facing community
college today. This constant barrage of hardships and trials can be discouraging. These presidents like the challenges they are facing.

> *I like a challenge. This presidency will be a challenging position for a long time*
> *and I like that.*

Just as the presidents were not motivated by money, power, control, or the
title to become a president, money, power, and the title are not the reasons
they remain a president. They are motivated by making a difference in the
lives of all students. They want to redesign community colleges to assist in
building healthy families and communities, and bring about transformational
change for the country. These are the reasons they remain in the leadership
position.

Vital to Our Country

Community colleges are vital institutions to the growth and well-being of
the United States. These institutions are as diverse as the communities and
students they serve. The one constant in today's community college environment is change. Gen X presidents embrace the ambiguity, the new challenges,
and the desire to revitalize their institutions to meet the changing needs of
our nation.

- *I believe in the work we are doing. Never have community colleges been*
  more important for our country. It is so much more than a paycheck. We
  serve students least likely to attend and the ones who will benefit the most.
  This is the most meaningful work. I love this work.
- *Community colleges are the vehicle for transformational changes in this*
  country.

- *Community colleges are great places for everyone and not just specific people. There is a place for all people to improve their lives and our country.*
- *Our graduating student cohort must mirror the communities we serve. Community colleges are the only institutions that can change the growing income gap.*

Commitment to the Local Community

Community colleges have multiple missions as they serve students, employers, and their local communities. The multiplicity of types of community colleges is directly related to the diversity of the local communities they serve. This variety is a key element in the value and return on investment of community colleges. Gen X presidents recognize the importance of the local community and express their commitment to bringing economic, social, and educational benefit to the citizens.

- *Being a rural community college president is important to who I am and who I want to be. My community needs me. This is bigger than my career. This is about the community and the college. The perception is the community exists because of the college.*
- *I have a passion for cultivating a college-going culture in the community. This is based on the power of higher education in improving economic opportunities for individuals and families.*
- *I have no desire to move on. I am committed to this community. The reason I do this job is not for the money or control or authority. It is about a passion for making a difference. Bringing in lots of resources to make a difference.*
- *I connect with community college work. I love to share the power or education with others. As a president, I am focused on external things as well as impacting the internal college community.*
- *Decisions the president makes impacts the entire community for generations to come. Nothing is more powerful.*

Students at the Center

A resounding theme throughout the interviews was students at the core of their presidential work. A genuine concern for students is articulated that is not simply an abstract concept. The presidents reflected upon getting to know individual students and spending time talking with students. The focus is on access into college and success of a college credential and/or transfer to a university for all students.

- *Whether I am in the community talking with board members of the symphony, CEOs of businesses, raising money for scholarships, or internally talking with faculty members or students, the message is always to help students learn. I am here to make a difference in the lives of students.*
- *The role of community college and its leadership is to help students gain access or admission into college, obtain sufficient financial aid, overcome personal challenges, academically succeed, and to graduate or help them transfer to a 4-year institution in a timely manner, all in an effort to help students reap the benefits of a college degree.*

Student success and completion is not a catch phrase. Student completion is something these presidents think about almost every day. Barriers in college processes that are impeding student completion is a concern.

- *I want to change the system so students do not see barriers.*
- *I love this job. I am in my second presidency. I was a campus president and now I report to a board. I am in it for the students. Each day I take 4 or 5 moments to reflect on how to make the college better for students. For example, why is it easier to withdraw from college than to enroll? My focus remains on students and the mission.*

Student success was defined as both completion and student learning. There was an expressed realization that a credential without skills and knowledge will not provide the foundation for a better life for students and their families.

- *I want to help all students learn. I am here to make a difference in the lives of students and prepare an environment for all students to be successful.*
- *The reward for the long hours and tough decisions comes when students succeed.*

The tassel is worth the hassle.

Impact

When examining the motivation for becoming a college president, our interviews revealed that chief among the reasons Gen Xers choose to take on these roles is because they want to make an impact on a large scale. These presidents express this same motivation for continuing to be a president although it is much more nuanced and intertwined within the larger context of other themes. Repetition of the statements earlier in this chapter regarding impact is not required here but a few comments about impact now that they are presidents are provided.

- *I have a broad sweeping influence and I impact many lives.*
- *If you want a job to make a difference then this is the job for you.*
- *Gen Xers want to feel we are part of something bigger than ourselves. Being a community college president allows me to satisfy that need.*
- *As a president. I can reach scale. By being a president I effect thousands of students, employees, and the community. I believe I make a difference.*

It Is Not Just Me

Gen X presidents stressed they cannot do this job alone. They know they do not work in a vacuum. They understand the need to assemble teams who are willing to represent the college and be involved with donors and legislators. They surround themselves with smart people and believe part of their responsibility as a president is to develop a tight-knit executive team and bring people together. They enjoy working with people and that contributes to their ability to stay and be successful.

- *This job is for people who enjoy being around people.*
- *I want to make a difference and influence change. I wanted the opportunity to help create the reality of a great team.*
- *I rely on relationships to get the job done not just to get the job.*

Having people informed about decision making and believing that everyone in the institution is important in moving the institution forward is a point espoused by this generation. An interesting phenomenon articulated by four presidents was eliminating most standing committees and bringing the right people together at the right time to address the issue or task at hand.

- *Standing committees do not make sense with the fast pace of change. With each issue that comes along I get the right people in the room regardless of their position at the college and we work to solve the problem.*
- *Committees are not effective if the same people are on the same committee for many years. Sure, there are some committees that are required such as accreditation but these are not ongoing year after year. I think having a more dynamic approach to creating teams around issues makes more sense today.*

Faculty

Gen X presidents know that to successfully address the challenges facing community colleges today, faculty must be an integral part of the solutions. Working with talented faculty encourages presidents to stay in their position.

Engaging faculty and encouraging their leadership can go from tribulation to triumph for these leaders.

- *The hardest work is not the external work with community and legislators. The hardest is to work with faculty on quality of life and workload issues. You have to shower love on faculty and staff.*
- *Faculty can be mean but they need someone to love and commit to them. (Like others, our college has had many presidential transitions in the last twenty years.) Faculty are impacting students' lives forever. They need to know the president is committed to the college and recognizes their contribution to the college.*

Sometimes faculty head in the wrong direction and presidents are compelled to make certain the focus on students is paramount. The redirection can be difficult but critical to accomplishing the mission of the college.

- *Faculty are entrenched and when you challenge them civility is a real issue. There are attacks on executives. Be prepared to navigate with diplomacy and tact as you address fundamental issues.*
- *The presidency has not been easy or smooth. Students do not have a foundation from the family. Our society has a generation who did not have expectations of civility and respect. I have to stand up for what is in the best interest of students even if faculty do not understand "no" and throw a tantrum. Even if this leads to a vote of no confidence, it is important to keep the focus on students. I tell faculty that if they disrespect me what will they do to students. My goal is to build bridges between faculty and administrators. Because of their interaction, people's lives will be changed forever.*

Enjoy the Work

Finally, Generation X presidents like the work of the presidency. The reasons for becoming a president were to make an impact and for the actual work rather than for the money or power of the position. Now that they are presidents, they find reward and joy in the work of the presidency and hence stay in the leadership position.

- *This job is the coolest job ever. I am energized in coming to work every day. I can make a difference.*
- *I moved from a small college to a large multi-campus district. I feel completely at home in both presidencies. I am energized by the work. Ambiguity of the job can be intimidating but I am so happy where I am.*
- *This is the most fulfilling thing. Being called president feels nice, too.*

- *This is my life's work and brings me a lot of joy. I find it rewarding and challenging I have learned some hard lessons. Like most Gen Xers, I am resilient and independent. I get both intrinsic and extrinsic rewards from helping students and changing generational poverty.*

These five reasons were reported by the Generation X presidents as critical for remaining in the leadership positions.

1. Community colleges are vital to the future of the United States.
2. Community colleges are vital to the economic, social, and educational benefit of the local community.
3. Students are at the center of the mission of the college and the work of the president.
4. The presidential position affords the opportunity for the leader to have impact on a larger scale.
5. The presidential position provides the opportunity to create a tight-knit executive team and engage faculty.

There were other reasons for becoming and staying a college president. Generation X presidents are individuals and do approach their work with divergent skills and talents. The themes identified in this chapter were resoundingly paramount among all the interviewed presidents.

The Right People in the Same Space at the Same Time
Thom D. Chesney

At one institution, for example, I discovered that the facilities team was across the board long-serving and of the same generation. Student life was similarly homogenous, but to the other extreme—no one over two years on the job, and all but one of them a Millennial. As I went about creating listening opportunities, I broke up and reconstituted groups like these and others similarly situated into ones which, consequently were more age and work group diverse. The outcomes exceeded my expectations. In one respect, I achieved what I had initially hoped for—a richer variety of perspectives and recommendations on my curiosity questions about how the college worked, what might be improved, and what I should preserve at all costs—"the best of our institutional DNA," as one speaker put it.

Beyond that, I also discovered that in one session after another that many attendees had never previously met with the president or met most of the others in the group, or both. However, they shared with equal frequency and urgency that they deeply valued their work family. So, on the one hand, I had revealed the generally siloed organizational structure I had inherited; on the other, I had discovered that for the most part people were comfortable within it.

When the listening sessions were concluded—with the additional promise that I would always be listening to learn—and we moved on to the vital work of crafting and affirming the college's first ever set of core values and a new strategic plan and vision, I returned to my experience of the first few months. The ideation and planning sessions were purposefully composed to be diverse in age, ethnicity, work role, and length of service. In the two-day off-site compression planning event that ultimately led to a new set of strategic priorities and immediate actions to begin achieving them, we had a 4-month employee seated adjacent to a 40-year one—and just about everything in between. It ultimately became a touchstone for nearly every one of the 25 colleagues who attended—a turning point we years later still refer to as when we decided not only to become "the college that finds people when and where they need us most," but also where our first response to every inquiry would be, "Here's how we can (or might) do that for you."

Do not think for a moment that everyone at the college agreed with the approach to the outcomes of "The December 25." Recalling the DNA comment from my listening tour, I was prepared to respond to critics of the process in particular because it was unlike any that my predecessors had undertaken. I brought in an outside group—the same one that had helped guide a similar process for our Board of Trustees—and personally selected all the participants rather than requesting volunteers, reserving slots for the historical participants, or both.

When asked why a certain senior leader who "had arrived with the bricks" was not included on the invitation list group, I shared in detail how invaluable her insight, input, and influence had been in guiding us to the many successes and achievements of the first four decades, and that we would carry forward the best of that work into the next forty years. I added that she would and should expect as much from us. As there could not be a seat at the table for every council and committee chair, senior faculty, staff, or administrator; or eager and willing volunteer, I planned the participant list to be as inclusive and representative as possible of all roles at the college and with special attention to individuals who I thought were most likely to stay around long enough to act in the short and long term on the decisions and recommendations which emerged from the planning session. As difficult and time consuming as it was to embark upon and defend the process, it was essential, and today hardly anyone is surprised when I call a meeting of "the right people in the same space at the same time" to solve a problem or celebrate the solution.

Chapter Four

Being Called to the Presidency During Tumultuous Times

Kathleen Plinske

The community college presidency represents an amazing opportunity to make a tremendous difference and impact in the community that the college serves. Along with that opportunity comes an awesome, almost burdensome, sense of responsibility. The work of community colleges is simply too critical and too urgent to not get right. We must find ways to raise the aspirations of our community, to increase access to higher education, to improve levels of student success, and to transform our workforce all while dealing with shrinking budgets, increased regulation, changing labor models, and greater scrutiny. As a young president, this confluence of pressures can initially appear overwhelming. However, there are several strategies that can help bring clarity to the challenging role of the presidency.

DO THE RIGHT THING FOR THE RIGHT REASON

As a new president, you may feel tremendous pressure to keep each of the college's many constituencies happy with your decisions. You tend to question each decision you are faced with:

1. If you don't renew this underperforming individual's contract, won't the union be upset with you?
2. If you sunset this underperforming and costly program won't the faculty be upset with you?
3. If you don't go along with this unrealistic proposal, won't the Board be upset with you?

After wrestling with these types of questions, feeling like every decision is a no-win situation, you should also wonder: "But if you don't make this difficult decision, won't students ultimately suffer as a result?" Rather than attempting to prevent others from being unhappy with you, you must discover that the most satisfying criterion for decision making is simply to do the right thing for the right reason. If a decision seems attractive because it would likely increase your popularity, you can discard that option because it probably isn't the right thing for the right reason. If a decision seems attractive because it represents the path of least resistance, then it likely is not the right thing for the right reason.

One of the very first things that you must learn as president is that it is entirely impossible to make everyone happy. No matter how much you analyze a decision and commit to selecting the best possible outcome, it is inevitable that someone will either be unhappy or will disagree with your decision. It is a fool's folly to believe that a utopian decision exists, and trying to find the solution that will make everyone happy is nothing but a waste of time.

Ultimately, keeping students' interests first and foremost in every decision reduces much of the agony in choosing between multiple options. While most decisions that reach the president are inevitably lose–lose decisions (the issues with obvious solutions are solved long before they reach you), choosing to do the right thing for the right reason often helps you sort through myriad possibilities and solutions.

Don't Try to Act Like a President

In addition to agonizing over many decisions, a new president may be challenged to try to determine how one is supposed to act as president. The question of wondering how a "real" president is supposed to act may ruminate. It may be comforting to know there is not a uniform description of how a president is supposed to act.

> *Only after several months of trying to be "presidential," I came to realize I couldn't separate myself from who I was. One breakthrough came when I was advised that I didn't have to worry about being too young to be the president; after all, everyone else would be worried about that for me. While initially it was embarrassing when community members who I had not yet met assumed I was head of the Student Government Association when I was introduced as president, I've come to learn that being a young president has its advantages, including seeming very approachable to students.*

Accept that *you* are the president and that you inherently bring *your identity* to the role. The sooner you do this, the sooner you will feel at ease in your position. You cannot separate who you are from the position you hold, and you should not try to. Creating a separate persona for yourself while you are on the job will limit your ability to lead from a place of authenticity. And the reality is, you are on the job all the time. Once appointed, you cannot escape the role of the presidency, so you might as well bring yourself, your entire self, to the role.

Find a Mentor Outside the Institution

As a newly appointed president, you suddenly find yourself with no peers at the institution. While a strong executive team and a supportive Board can help reduce feelings of isolation, the fact remains that every employee at the college ultimately reports to you and every trustee ultimately supervises you. The role of president can often be lonely, and there will be times when a confidant outside of the college will be an exceedingly valuable ally.

Less than two weeks after assuming my role as interim president, I found myself desperately in need of advice. As I walked onto campus, I was not surprised to see a line of students outside Student Services because it was the first day of spring registration. However, I was shocked to see a line of several hundred students lined up throughout the atrium. As I walked up and down the line of students to address their concerns and frustrations, I learned that our online course registration system had crashed.

As I listened to students' complaints about missing class in order to wait in line to register for next semester, I was approached by a number of employees who wanted to know why their paychecks hadn't yet been posted to their bank accounts. After a quick visit to the finance office, I discovered that our staff had made a critical oversight in the previous evening's payroll process, resulting in the payroll file not having been properly posted to the bank.

My immediate response to both situations was to make sure that our students and employees were taken care of. That included manually protecting students' spring course schedules as well as staying overnight to hand-deliver checks to the third-shift staff. However, I felt the need to talk with someone about what had happened, and at that point, I didn't know who I could trust.

Fortunately, the highly experienced interim president whom the Board originally hired to serve for a year agreed to be my mentor. It was reassuring to have someone outside the college with whom to debrief. I was able to brainstorm with someone who didn't have a vested interest in institutional politics, or an agenda that might conflict with the appropriate response to addressing these systematic failures.

Learn to Improvise

There is no prescripted solution in response to your registration system crashing on the same day you miss payroll. There is no instruction manual for the myriad challenges a president faces. Rather, a successful president is often called upon to be an artful improviser, and sometimes you must "fake it 'til you make it." The role of the president is to consider all facets of the situation at hand and determine the best course of action given the information available at the time.

It may be tempting to think that you are not yet ready for the role of the presidency because you haven't yet experienced all situations presidents might find themselves in. While you can learn by observing a president from the ranks of the executive team, there is simply no substitute for being the one who ultimately has to make the final difficult decisions. Just as you can learn a lot about improvisation from watching and observing a jazz pianist, nothing can fully prepare you for the experience of putting *your* fingers to the keys. Ultimately, nothing can fully prepare you for all the difficult decisions you will have to make as the president.

Keep the Main Thing the Main Thing

Despite the turmoil that may be happening at the college, a reassuring event regularly happens: students walk through the doors, they attend classes, and they learn. An important role of the president is to deflect the distractions that can find their way into the college, and allow faculty and staff to focus on serving students. While the distractions can sometimes make it easy to "major in minor things," it is important to keep the main thing the main thing, and in the case of a community college presidency, the main thing must always be student learning.

Find time to get out of your office and interact with students. Despite the challenges that you may face on any given day, make time to connect with students, learn their stories, and understand how the college is encouraging them to pursue their dreams. It is the best antidote to the stress that is inherent in senior leadership. Teaching a course each semester is perhaps the ideal way to maintain an authentic connection with students as well as to understand and empathize with the challenges that faculty routinely face. However you choose to do it, making sure to stay connected to the heart of the college and the core of your work is critical.

SO, WHAT DOES A COMMUNITY COLLEGE PRESIDENT ACTUALLY DO?

When the Board was about to appoint me as interim president, one of the Trustees, in a public meeting, declared: "If we are going to name a 29-year-old as president, we must send her to 'finishing school'." The "finishing school" selected for me was the League for Innovation's Executive Leadership Institute.

There, I met Dr. Sandy Shugart and learned about his leadership at Valencia College, which serves Orange and Osceola counties in Florida. As I listened to him speak about Valencia, I dreamt about what it might be like to work at a place like that. Fortunately, after I fulfilled my nine-month role as interim president, I had the opportunity to join Valencia as campus president.

Dr. Shugart advises that each presidency you hold creates a story, and it is important to determine what story you want told at the end of your presidency. Some presidencies are stories of managing enrollment growth, expanding to meet a community's growing needs. Some presidencies are stories of transition, leading the institution to a new place to meet changing needs. A few presidencies, the most special and carefully crafted presidencies, are stories of the creation of remarkable learning environments that dramatically improve student success. His advice was clear: be careful in crafting the story of your presidency.

I believed my role as interim president at McHenry County College was to restore a level of stability to the institution, yet this felt like a wholly unsatisfactory answer to the question "What exactly is a community college president supposed to do?" Through the work of crafting the story of my campus presidency at Valencia College, I began to find what felt like acceptable answers to that question.

Dream Big Dreams

In 2011, Osceola County had one of the lowest college-going rates in the state of Florida, ranking fifty-seventh out of sixty-seven counties. After partnering with the superintendent of the School District and the county's Education Foundation, we established the bold goal of increasing the county's college-going rate to be the top in the state. Together with the community we are working to identify and remove the barriers that prevent students from going to college. Over the last five years we have seen a steady increase in the county's college-going rate.

While it would have been safer to set our goal to increase the college-going rate to match the state average, it is unlikely that such a goal would have created as much excitement in the community. Many community leaders now believe in the transformational power of significantly increasing the college-going rate and have genuinely embraced this bold goal.

Your role as president is not to simply maintain and protect the status quo. Rather, you play a critical role in painting a bold and aspirational vision of what the future could be. As a key leader in the community, you have the responsibility to articulate the remarkable possibilities that could result from achieving extraordinary success. In fact, perhaps the most dangerous thing

that you can do is to set small, easily attainable goals as they foster compla-
cency and limit ambition and innovation.

Give Voice to Students

A recent Valencia graduate requested an opportunity to meet to share his concerns about his experience transferring to the university. An undocumented
immigrant, he started at Valencia in 2007 as a senior in high school. He completed twenty-four credit hours via dual enrollment, but could not afford to
continue in college after graduating from high school. Even though he had
lived in Florida since he was in elementary school, given his immigration
status, he would have been required to pay out-of-state tuition.

In 2014, after many of our students with similar stories lobbied for change,
a legislation was passed that allowed DREAMers to pay in-state tuition if
they had graduated from a Florida high school and had applied for admission
at a college or university within two years. After waiting seven years, this
particular student returned to Valencia and quickly completed his associate's
degree. However, when he attempted to transfer to the university, he was
told that he was not eligible to pay in-state tuition because he had applied to
Valencia *before* graduating from high school, rather than within two years
after having graduated, as the law stipulates. Valencia does not have a mecha-
nism for dual enrollment students to reapply after high school graduation
because they are already admitted and enrolled.

> *When the student shared his concerns with me, I reached out to a number of
> administrators who had high-level contacts at the university in an effort to over-
> turn the decision. Fortunately, he was ultimately allowed to pay in-state tuition
> at the university, but it gives me pause to think what would have happened to his
> dreams if we hadn't heard the details of his story and given him a voice.*

The majority of students at community colleges do not fit the standard
definition of a traditional student. And, as we reach students of more diverse
backgrounds, they tend to share less and less in common with the traditional
student model. However, many of our institutional processes, as well as state
and federal policies, have been designed to serve the needs of traditional
students. As president, you have the unique opportunity and responsibility
to give voice to those students for whom our traditional systems and models
do not fit.

By listening to your students' stories, and taking the time to understand the
unique obstacles and challenges they face, you often have the opportunity to
make a significant difference in your students' lives. Moreover, by working
to change the systems whose designs pose unintended consequences for students, your impact can spread beyond the confines of your institution.

Believe in Your Students

At Valencia, we are guided by a simple but powerful belief: "Anyone can learn anything under the right conditions." We reject the notion that there is an "algebra gene" and that the students who are missing that from their chromosomes will just never be able to solve for *x*. We refuse to believe that some students are not cut out to be good writers or just do not have what it takes to succeed in college. Rather, we acknowledge that students must work hard toward their academic endeavors, and we believe that we must work hard to identify and create those conditions that are most effective in helping students be successful in their pursuit of learning.

> *Early in my role at Valencia, I met a student who required developmental coursework in reading, writing, and mathematics. The five-year graduation rate for students with this level of remediation need hovers around 15percent. If this were not enough, she did not have access to a car, and her commute to campus on the bus took two-and-a-half hours . . . each way. If anyone at the college believed that she was not "college material," she likely would have lived up to those expectations. However, her unrelenting spirit and dogged determination combined with caring faculty and staff who believed she could be successful, and helped her believe the same, allowed her to achieve her dream of earning her degree.*

One of your most important duties as president is to believe in your students and to expect them to amaze you in the most wonderful ways. Cynicism toward students has no place in the office of the president, for it is bound to be amplified throughout the institution. If faculty or staff suspect that you do not have faith in your students, why should they? And if faculty and staff stop believing in your students, you have no chance to implement any meaningful improvements to student learning.

It is an entirely different mindset to believe that all students can learn anything, rather than to wish students were better prepared, to wish they all spoke English as their native language, or to wish that their third-grade math teachers had done a better job explaining fractions a decade ago. It is a mindset that does not allow you to simply "write off" students for whom the odds seem too high.

Develop a Rock Star Team

Your team will have a significant impact on your success as president. It is imperative that you not only establish a highly talented and committed leadership team, but also that you set the expectation of hiring "rock stars" throughout the college. Often, one of the most important hiring decisions you can make is to not make a decision at all; in other words, if the right candidate is not in the applicant pool, do not extend an offer. Because of the perceived cost to the search committee to declare a search a failure, it is far too common to settle for a candidate who does not bring exactly the right qualities to the position. However, the cost of selecting a candidate who is not the right fit is far more damaging in the long run.

Again—Keep the Main Thing the Main Thing

One of the most interesting facets of the community college presidency is that no two days are the same. Each day brings its own unique set of opportunities and challenges. However, regardless of what each day brings, it is critical to keep the needs and interests of our students first. The words of Dr. Larry W. Tyree, a long-time and highly successful community college president, serve as a powerful reminder of how to "keep the main thing the main thing."

A student is...
The most important person on the campus. Without students there would be no need for the institution.
Not a cold enrollment statistic, but a flesh and blood human being with feelings and emotions like our own.
Not someone to be tolerated so that we can do our thing. They are our thing.
Not dependent on us. Rather, we are dependent on them.
Not an interruption of our work, but the purpose of it. We are not doing a favor by serving them. They are doing us a favor by giving us the opportunity to do so.

Getting the Call
Kathleen Plinske

On October 19, 2009, at the ripe old age of 29, I became interim president of McHenry County College, a community college located in the suburbs of Chicago. As I drove to work on my first day as interim president, two thoughts went through my mind: one, "While I had declared I wanted to one day be a community college president, I really didn't mean now," and two, "I wonder what exactly a community college is supposed to do?"

My pathway to a college presidency was atypical by all measures. In 2001, a week after graduating with a bachelor's degree in Spanish and physics, I was hired at McHenry County College as an instructional media specialist to assist faculty with online course development. Over the next eight years, I earned a master's and doctorate while continuing to work full-time, and held seven different positions at the college, each with increasing levels of responsibility. I had been interested in a career pathway that would eventually lead to a community college presidency, but considered it a long-term goal.

In February 2009, at a special meeting called by the Board of Trustees, the Board and the president reached an agreement whereby the president would immediately step down from his post. With no clear succession plan in place, the Board appointed the interim vice president of academic affairs to serve as interim president, even though he had already announced his plans to retire within four months. When he retired as scheduled, the Board appointed as interim president the CFO, who promptly announced that he had taken another job and gave his two weeks' notice.

In the meantime, the Board had been recruiting an external candidate to serve as interim president while it conducted a formal search process for a replacement president. Although the Board hired a highly successful and experienced external candidate to serve as interim president for one year, he announced after one month on the job that he had decided to resign. So, at the age of 29 and with eight years of experience at the college, I was the senior member of the executive team and was the next one to be called upon to serve as interim president.

When I learned that the Board was going to ask me to serve as interim president, I remember thinking that the circumstances were certainly far from ideal. I was concerned about my likelihood of success as the fifth president in a period of eight months. I also remember wondering if my career aspirations were misguided: "Why would I want this job if it turned out so badly for my predecessors?"

The outgoing interim president worked to convince me that I was the best candidate for the position, despite my feeling totally overwhelmed and completely out of my league. At a minimum, he convinced me that I was the only internal candidate left! As a native of the area, I felt a strong calling and a commitment to the college's mission of service to its students and the community. Out of this sense of duty to the college and to the students, I accepted the position.

At the time it felt like I was being thrown into the ocean as shark bait. As I reflect on the experience, I realize it was more like diving into the deep end of the pool—while such an experience is scary, you ultimately learn to swim, and you may even learn to love swimming. My experience as interim president taught me a number of critical lessons that continue to serve me well.

Chapter Five

Intrusive Mentoring

Linda L. García

Generation X community college presidents who were interviewed for this book believe their mentors had a significant role in their career path leading to the presidency. They felt if it were not for their mentors saying *"You are ready. I see this in you. Take the plunge,"* then they may have never pursued the position. Thus, this experience convinces them that a deeper type of mentoring—intrusive mentoring—is necessary to positively influence individuals into this position.

Mentoring is a "relationship between teacher (mentor) and pupil (protégé) that facilitates learning" (McDade 2005, 760). It has also been defined to be a "professionally centered relationship between two individuals in which the more experienced individual, the mentor, guides, advises, and assists in the career of the less experienced protégé" (VanDerLinden 2005, 737). Kram and Isabella (1985, 111) refer to mentoring as providing less experienced individuals with "career-enhancing functions, such as sponsorship, coaching, facilitating exposure and visibility, and offering challenging work or protection, all of which help the . . . person to establish a role in the organization, learn the ropes, and prepare for advancement." Frequently, the process to identify a mentor will start with the protégé or less experienced individual seeking a person who will eventually evolve to become a mentor.

Intrusive mentoring takes mentoring a step further. Intrusive mentoring is a more proactive and strategic type of mentorship. It requires more than occasional interactions between a mentor and a protégé. Intrusive mentoring occurs when a soon-to-be mentor identifies a person who shows potential for leadership advancement—the community college presidency in this case. This mentor approaches that person, introduces the concept of the presidency role as a future career advancement, and provides planned support to increase the capability and confidence of the protégé to prepare and fulfill the role.

The concept of intrusive mentoring is on the rise as soon-to-be retired community college presidents and other community college leaders feel an obligation to prepare for the next generation of leaders. They are alarmed that "the pool of potential applicants for the CEO positions being hired is shrinking" (AACC 2013, 3), especially "one in four of the country's 1,132 community colleges experience some type of leadership transition" (Smith 2016). Community college leaders view the leadership shortage as a threat to the future of the community college sector and achieving student success. Thus, they are motivated to become mentors and strategically identify and help prepare the next generation of leaders fill the upcoming vacancies.

The community college presidents interviewed for this book described the intrusive mentoring experience:

- *I had a mentor say to me, "I don't know why you are pursing sociology. You are going to be a community college president." This impressed me. I was stunned.*
- *I always thought I would be a partner in a CPA firm. However, two years into working at this college there was an opportunity to be the next president. Someone said I should do it. I was not considering this at all.*
- *I received early encouragement from a dissertation advisor who told me, "You will make a great college president." It was odd because I was reaching a milestone to be a professor.*
- *My president put a bug in my ear when she started a sentence with "When you are the president." That caught me off guard in a positive way. I had no plans to be a community college president.*
- *The former interim president told the board that I should be the next president of the campus. I was shocked by the statement. I thought I still needed a lot of learning to do.*

The mentor's approach to "plant a seed" and empower the protégés to seek the community college presidency initially created mixed feelings for the current presidents:

> *This sounds crazy. Can I really do this job? Do I have the skills? Why me? I want a balanced life, and I don't think the community college presidency is that. Well, maybe I can actually do this—be a community college president. But, I didn't plan for this.*

IS IT RIGHT FOR ME?

Even though the mentors believed the community college presidency was right for these individuals, the current presidents stressed the importance of also knowing their personal values before pursing the role—*"Ask yourself why you want to do this. Do serious soul searching. Do you see this to fulfill a mission in life? Be honest on what is important to you."* The presidents shared their perspectives of the job demands when assessing if the community college president role is the right career path:

- *Know that you are always the president and you have to accept that. You have to be presentable at all times. I know it's funny, but presentation is important. Your energy can't be low. If it is, then the job will eat you for lunch. If you can't handle a multiple of activities in a day, then this job is not for you.*
- *Know on any given day, you won't be embraced by everyone. You can't satisfy all groups. There are many groups you have to satisfy (community, campus, staff, etc.). They all need attention. You have to have the moral compassion in you so you can look at yourself and know you will be okay. You need that inner strength. Look within you. You need to be resilient.*
- *You need to ask them (individuals considering the role) if they enjoy drinking from 25 firehoses (figuratively speaking)! As a president, you are going in different directions all the time in a day (rotary, curriculum student issues, etc.). If you like structure, then the job is not for you. You have to enjoy being around people. And, if you want a job to make a difference, then this is the job for you!*
- *You have to be okay with that huge learning curve when you start the president role, especially to work with academics, finances, politics, and accreditation. You need to be a huge risk taker.*
- *Know that the job is never complete. Sometimes projects are never ending because they continue to evolve. You have to be comfortable with that.*
- *There are discouraging and fulfilling moments about the presidency. I would hear other presidents say about other presidents, "You should never do that as a president" or "that's not presidential." You can let these conversations overwhelm you.*

PREPARING FOR THE ROLE

Preparing for the community college presidency can be an overwhelming experience, especially with this first thought—*Where do I start? How do I begin to prepare?* The best advice the presidents received from their mentors was to begin seeking extra leadership responsibilities, such as volunteering to lead strategic initiatives, when considering and preparing for the community college president role.

The presidency is hard work. Seek opportunities to help you strengthen your skills. Look at opportunities to improve situations such as joining or chairing an accreditation committee or strengthening the student success outcomes for your college. Take on those initiatives. Show you can create a strategic plan and accomplish it.

Additional advice from mentors included seeking other mentors who have different leadership styles and who can provide new learning experiences.

- *Learn to implement what you love from a variety of mentors. Take pieces from everyone. Engage with people close to the position.*
- *Look for mentors at any age in the president position. Get to know what they do. There are good presidents that show action on what it takes to be a great president. They are people that just do.*
- *People need to be around and in front of presidents to get an understanding of the job.*
- *I ask a lot of people to help me and be my mentor, especially from people who are in my boss's shoes. I have mentors who are my age too. I want to be in a space with people I aspire to be.*
- *Someone told me to ask a president to be a mentor. I wasn't feeling comfortable to do this. But, the person said he would ask for me, and I would become embarrassed as it showed my shyness.*

Throughout the intrusive mentorship, the presidents shared there was a high level of commitment from their mentors such as providing exposure to certain activities and opportunities, developing professional networks, and becoming politically savvy.

Other recommendations included earning a doctorate degree and seeking professional development opportunities such as the American Association of Community College's John E. Roueche Future Leaders Institute, Aspen Presidential Fellowship for Community College Excellence, and the League for Innovation in the Community College's Executive Leadership Institute. A president mentioned, *"Achieving success takes planning and time. So, begin to prepare now!"*

PAYING IT FORWARD: TAPPING THE FUTURE ROCK STARS

The presidents shared their gratitude for the intrusive mentoring they received from their mentors as it positively changed their career path. This experience has influenced their thinking on how they can expand on this type of intrusive mentorship, especially exposing the talents of younger leaders.

- *We need to create opportunities for young leaders who are the upcoming rock stars. Sometimes human resource rules need to be bent to put them into the senior level positions. Who cares if a person doesn't have the five-year senior leadership requirement for a specific job. It's about fit. Colleges need to consider a person who has demonstrated that he or she can do it. Sometimes it's not about the years of experience.*
- *There are rock stars who are not involved in the national "in crowd." They don't get noticed. But, I believe it's the responsibility of us and future mentors to expose the young leaders. Young leaders don't know how to get in those crowds, so they feel they won't advance.*
- *We need conversations about succession planning and leadership and include the younger leaders in that discussion. There is so much talent at the mid-level management.*
- *We need younger leaders involved in national committees and participating in critical discussions on student success. A plan needs to be created on how to elevate young leaders for exposure.*

Strategically tapping future rock stars and alleviating barriers to the presidency is a major component of intrusive mentoring. It empowers the protégé to seek and pursue career advancement during a time when community college leaders are concerned on the lack of new leaders filling the community college president vacancies. "As a large percentage of senior community college administrators and leaders enter into retirement over the next decade . . . the college leaders must look critically at the available pool of potential leaders . . . to ensure the institution continues forward movement as the . . . community college leadership generation heads into retirement" (Strom, Sanchez and Downey-Schilling 2011, 19). Rabey (2001, 29) states, "It is important that the vast knowledge current community college presidents have be passed along to the next generation of leaders to ensure the community colleges continue to thrive."

Chapter Six

"The Real Work"

Gen X Presidents as Mentors for Student Success and Sustainability

JoAlice Blondin

Colleagues are a wonderful thing—but mentors, that's where the real work gets done.

—Junot Díaz

Members of Generation X have been variously described as "apathetic" or "cynical," and there is some truth to the "cynical" label. For Generation Xers, who witnessed iconic historic events ranging from the fall of the Berlin Wall to a rise in the divorce rate, the world was uncertain—and best approached with wariness and a sense of humor, and a very dry one at that. Gen Xers took nothing at face value. There was always a subtext, and we were going to go beneath the surface to find it.

Many Gen Xers will remember a popular bumper sticker from the eighties that read, "Question Authority," as though our entire generation was giving itself permission to ask the hard questions to parents, teachers, police officers, legislators, or even the President of the United States. The old way of doing things was not going to satisfy the keen and suspicious eyes of future Gen X leaders, and the questions started coming, starting as college students: "Why are classes scheduled on these specific days?" "Who is a bursar?" "How did you calculate the athletic fee?" This was an early indication of a Gen X college president in the making.

Gen Xers have also been described as "entrepreneurial," "flexible," and "balanced," perhaps as a result of these cultural and historic influences. Finding connections amid the uncertainty of the economic landscapes of the seventies and eighties may have led to these characteristics, as well as tackling and solving problems in groups rather than as individuals. Teamwork appealed to Gen Xers perhaps because we craved unity, and we also wanted to ensure the sustainability and redundancy of our efforts. We are nothing if not a practical generation.

Based on these observations, it comes as no surprise that Gen X community college presidents are actively engaged in mentoring the next group of community college leaders to ensure student success for generations to come, as well as smooth succession to the presidency for these leaders. Gen X presidents believe that the next generation of college presidents is part of the responsibility of the presidency. Gen X presidents' approach to mentoring is not unique, though in some key ways we differ greatly from their Baby Boomer predecessors. This chapter will illustrate these differences as well as offer advice to future community leaders on how to prepare for the presidency, Gen X-style. There is a high likelihood that any sitting Gen X president, while mentored by a Boomer president or leader, probably did not follow all the advice he or she was given.

There is no argument that the Baby Boomer presidents presided over countless community college successes during their tenure—and continued tenure—such as unprecedented growth in enrollments and program expansions, but through observing Baby Boomers' leadership style, Gen X presidents very respectfully but distinctively forged their own paths.

One of my mentors explained that the first year of any college presidency (what I refer to as Page One of The Book for New Presidents, Baby Boomer Edition*) is about listening. I don't disagree that listening is critical, but in this era of limited resources, performance-based funding, concerns about college affordability—or even the value of higher education—I felt the need to act that first year. Change was necessary in order to respond to the shifting environment and enrollments at community college in the post–Great Recession age, and I named this action "planned urgency."*

We needed to act quickly to respond to, for example, the comprehensive performance-based funding model implemented in Ohio. Change must be of the grassroots variety and could not be top down, or it never would be accepted.

I accelerated the strategic planning process, and used that process as a way to engage and familiarize myself with the faculty and staff, Board of Trustees, the community, legislators, and, of course, the students.

Page 1 of that fictitious book states that the strategic plan is at least one to two years after the first-year listening phase, which means that any fundamental, systemic change is two to three years away at the earliest. In the current environment, this is unacceptable.

I was at an impasse: should I follow my mentor's advice and "do as he did" or forge my own path and do what I felt was right instinctively? I chose the latter, and one of my first initiatives at Clark State—within the first two months—was the development of a comprehensive strategic plan, engaging all faculty and staff college-wide. Through this plan, all faculty and staff focused on a collective and shared vision for how to move the institution toward measurable increases in student success as well as revising our mission, vision, guiding principles, and planning goals. In doing so, I generated the "buy-in" necessary to move the plan forward as a result of joint ownership of the plan by faculty and staff as well as a renewal and investment in a new shared governance model that created a communication and accountability structure for the campus, and all within one year.

Needless to say, Gen X presidents take a new path when we develop as leaders. The following six characteristics demonstrate how Gen X presidents approach the community college presidency as leaders and mentors.

WE CREATE NEW MENTORSHIP MODELS

An informal but targeted and intentional mentoring process has evolved. Rather than embrace the past model of mentoring favored by Boomer colleagues, where individuals waited to be "tapped" or chosen as the next leader, look at the existing talent on campus and the data.

For talent, I had a brand new provost, and for data, I had declining course completion statistics.

Ohio community colleges receive 50 percent of their funding from the state based on course-level completion. At Clark State, in 2014, face-to-face course completion had fallen to 73 percent college-wide and 69 percent for online courses, and Board members, administrators, faculty, staff, and students alike all recognized the need to focus on increasing course completion rates. With a busy and often overcommitted faculty, this was going to be a challenge, and we did not have the resources to hire twenty completion coaches, or scale and make mandatory supplemental instruction overnight, but we had to act.

And did I mention I had a new provost? He needed the faculty and staff to support this effort and he needed the assistance of key influence leaders on campus to help make his, and the campus' case for course completion.

In looking at the data and the talent, identify an individual on campus who can assist you with the work. For example, at Clark State there was a long-time employee who was very gifted in her job and work with students, but was experiencing a level of burnout in her student affairs role. She had the support of and comfort level with the faculty, and would be a perfect fit in a role that supported the integration of academic initiatives with student affairs' operations. Mentoring this person to assist with a transition into a new role within academic affairs, which was not initially a promotion, could lead to increased responsibilities and a promotion.

Within two years, this individual became the Associate Dean of Academic Affairs because of her hard work, but also because she was co-mentored by the president and the provost. She also took on a mentoring-type role, called cross-mentoring, with the provost by assisting him in his transition at Clark State. This co- and cross-mentoring model works because Gen X presidents seek new ways of executing campus goals with excellence, as well as sharing the responsibility of mentoring as a way to benefit multiple employees. And Clark State is experiencing gains in its course completion rate as a result of this model and the Associate Dean's leadership and close work with the faculty and staff. This example represents "the real work" of mentoring, and the benefits to the college, the students, and the individuals involved.

WE ARE REFLEXIVELY COLLABORATIVE

The biggest difference between my Baby Boomer colleagues, particularly those who previously mentored Gen X presidents, is that Gen Xers are more collaborative. As Gen Xers, we recognize the need for collective buy-in on key decisions because we worked under the "top-down" model of our Boomer colleagues. Yes, there are some decisions that have to be and will be unilateral and do not involve our shared governance process, such as terminating an individual for stealing from the campus. Most decisions made on a daily basis, however, involve the administrative team, made up of a diverse group of vice presidents, chief officers, and directors.

A leadership team works together on the strategic direction of the campus as well as tactical decisions that are required of a variety of roles. A distributive leadership model ensures that decision-making authority is present and exercised throughout the campus. The president wants to guarantee that decisions that affect students are made quickly in order to help students quickly (see "planned urgency"), and that the faculty and staff are empowered to work on the campus's and students' behalves. However, this leadership model requires a great deal of training, time, investment, and tolerance of mistakes in order to be effective.

An example of distributive leadership is the "student walkthrough." Clark State's faculty and staff have participated in many "student walkthroughs," in which we improve services collectively to students by walking through an experience on campus through the eyes of student. All stakeholders are present at a walkthrough, which generally takes place every two months around an issue, such as admissions and enrollment.

When I first arrived at Clark State, I asked the question, "How many times does a student need to physically come to campus before s/he is sitting in class with his/her books?" The answer was ten. Ten times. Ten tanks of gas! Ten babysitters! But I didn't say that. Instead, I asked them to see through the eyes of student and walkthrough their processes. They identified the unnecessary or onerous steps, and worked together, across departments, to fix these issues for students. Now, it takes just three visits, because one of the areas identified was the online application process, which, if functional, would reduce the number of visits by half. I took that recommendation and found the resources to help our faculty and staff make that change. I guided and I listened, but the decision was theirs.

WE MAKE MISTAKES AND OWN THEM IMMEDIATELY

What happens when an individual you mentored makes a mistake, and it is a big mistake? For example, a mistake that costs the college a significant industry partnership—in a growing economic sector in the region. Of course, you are not happy. Gen X presidents generally care deeply for the faculty and staff, and take a position of support and caring to address the problems directly and immediately.

I found out about the situation because the individual I was mentoring came directly to me and laid out the issues: one of his direct reports had not followed up, and hence he hadn't followed up. He made the mistake of thinking that communication had taken place and the situation was being handled. I gently explained that, and walked him through a few ways to correct this situation, starting with scheduling a meeting with the industry partner management and including me, so that we can, together, emphasize how we might fix it and let the business know that we are willing to do so. He agreed to do this, as well as fix the other communication issues I had identified, and report back within a week. Next, he asked me how to handle the dean, and I encouraged him to handle the situation with her as I had with him.

WE TRY TO LOSE OUR EGOS

The first thing to remember is "Don't confuse who you are with the job you do." You have to have a "you" outside of work. The very worst thing you can do is go home and be president of your house. You need to create balance and separate yourself from the job, which goes without saying, and the added benefit is that you cannot take anything personally. When someone attacks the college, this person is not attacking you.

By the same token, you may witness many a Boomer president suffer as a result of insults, bad press, or faculty and staff discontent because they associated their identities and egos so closely with the presidency. This association led some of these leaders to let professional decisions become personal, and this conflation of the personal and professional can be disastrous.

I witnessed a president, early in my career as an English professor, take the criticism of faculty members about workload issues so personally that he scheduled mandatory meetings with these faculty members and interrogated them based on gossip, rumor, and innuendo. He was never taken seriously, because the faculty and staff perceived that he wasn't taking the business of the college seriously. Rather, he lost any authority or power as a result of confusing who he was with the job he was doing. He also forgot the big picture: students.

Another way Gen X presidents attempt to "lose our egos" is by forgoing some of the traditional elements of the college presidency. For example, many boards (and the newly hired president) want to have an investiture or installation ceremony for the new president. Steer clear of this "ephemera of the office," regardless of the role you are in. Instead, invest the resources—money, staff time, and real time—in creating a student success agenda.

I wanted the monies set aside for my investiture to be designated for student scholarships.

Or take the "Welcome Back" reception monies for faculty and staff and host a student success summit, or a student event that focuses on completion. As an aspiring president, begin forgoing these trappings at all levels, and turn your resources into student successes.

Lastly, "losing your ego" means finding your replacement, which means admitting that you are replaceable. All the success you create as a president should be credited to the board, the faculty, the staff, and the students, so succession planning is a natural extension of this critical campus need. Chances are the campus has a disaster recovery plan, but training up the next president? Probably not, as most new presidents and their boards do not consider succession planning as critical.

Succession planning is a charge presidents need to begin on day 1: find a competent and trustworthy individual who can fill your role should something happen to you, and then work on finding your replacement, and mentoring that individual or individuals, for the next several years. A president needs to be open about this succession planning process with the Board of Trustees, the faculty and staff, ensuring the continuation of the student success agenda that is paramount to the institution's health and sustainability.

> *I identified two individuals, within my first month, who could, if called upon, take over the duties of the presidency on an interim basis. These were long-serving and seasoned individuals who I trusted and who the Board knew and trusted.*

Next, look for your replacement.

> *When I was at the Ozark Campus of Arkansas Tech, I decided to hire a Chief Academic Officer who could function as my replacement, and I did the same at Clark State.*

Moreover, begin intensive team-building activities with the leadership team and the co-mentoring model discussed earlier to ensure cross-training in each functional area, but also personal growth for each leader to design a unique career path for each.

WE ARE AUTHENTIC

Most of us have known a president that prides himself on his remoteness. He cultivated an air of mystery, which in turn invites the faculty, staff, and students to create their own version of his personality. In their version, this remoteness translated to authoritarianism and a lack of investment in the institution, and the air of mystery meant that he lacked a personal touch. While none of this was true, the perception of their leader as disengaged was more powerful than the reality that he cared deeply about the institution. He was told by his mentor to keep his personality out of the job, which is often heard from my Boomer mentors. Never share too much about your personal life, or show who you really are as a person, because that always gets you in trouble.

> • *One of my mentors, who knew that the above advice simply wasn't possible or workable for me, told me to always be myself, or I would be uncomfortable playing the role of the remote president. He explained to me, as I do now to anyone I mentor, that rather than detracting from my leadership ability, that my empathy, sense of humor, and personal approach are what would make me a good president. He once asked me what I thought my biggest strength as a leader was, and I replied, "I'm authentic. I can't be like those*

other leaders, who never crack a smile." I knew I was exaggerating, but he
assured me that I didn't have to be that way. I know it is cliché, but he told
me to be myself.

Sometimes we do need that permission to be ourselves, and many Boards, faculty, staff, and students are not used to the openness that Gen Xers bring to community college leadership. While many presidents embrace social media, Gen X presidents employ a host of communication tools to ensure that we get our message to our stakeholders and that these stakeholders can communicate with us: Twitter, blogging, e-mail, regular mail, hard copy newsletters, websites, newspaper columns, trade organizations, or town hall meetings. As stated earlier, the biggest mistake anyone can make is to assume that communication happened. A multipronged communication strategy with a feedback loop built in is absolutely essential for any president to be successful and is invaluable for campus morale.

WE ARE NOT SURE WE NEED ALL THIS SPACE AND WE DO NOT WANT MORE

Funding models and state support for community colleges have changed drastically over the years, and the only certainty is that of unpredictability. At the same time that state and local funding for higher education has been, for the most part, decreasing, enrollments at community colleges have leveled off or, in some cases, declined. Gen X presidents are contending with aging physical plants, with many buildings reaching forty to fifty years old, coupled with a technology infrastructure that is need of serious investment. In addition, many students have migrated to online or technology-enhanced education. At institutions, nearly 50 percent of students take at least one online class.

Changes in building use and viability over the past decade call into question the need for new and better buildings. Baby Boomer presidents, of both four and two-year institutions, demonstrated progress during their tenures by expanding the campus footprint and building. Gen X presidents are concerned with sustainability of the existing infrastructure and a serious need to improve technology and the student experience.

Gen X presidents have a more challenging task to donors, legislators, students, faculty, staff, and Boards of Trustees in selling increases in technology and an improved student experience rather than a new building, complete with classrooms ready for naming. Articulating the reasons why the college needs investment in existing facilities and services as opposed to new building is indeed difficult, but best explained by the shift from access and enrollment to success and completion.

This shift perfectly typifies the Gen X presidents' challenge, and the lesson to those we mentor. We believe in outputs rather than inputs, with the output being the investment we make. This is not to imply that a new building is not important to student success and moving the college forward, but is it always necessary? Gen X presidents and those we mentor must ask that question.

All community college presidents put students first. While generational differences may affect the way presidents conduct business, the goal is to provide students with access to affordable, quality education, and do everything possible to help them achieve their educational goals. Gen X presidents know that the future of higher education will be created by those we mentor, whether it is through the co-mentoring model, leadership institutes, doctoral programs, or informal mentoring relationships. It is time for Gen X presidents to identify those leaders and do everything possible to train, support, and nurture the next generation of community college presidents.

Chapter Seven

New Strategic Planning

Kirk A. Nooks

This book is about Generation X presidents and their perspective on a number of various topics or approaches. This chapter will cover the general topic of strategic planning. However, this chapter is not about how Generation X presidents are the first to use strategic planning. The concept of strategic planning in colleges and universities has been around since the founding of Harvard College in 1636. Whether he called it strategic planning or survival, Harvard's first president, Henry Dunster, was credited with taking several strategic steps to benefit the burgeoning institution in the short- and long-term.

He led the charge to build some of the institution's first structures, drafted the documents to incorporate and advance the concept of a four-year (vs. three-year) college experience. Dunster was also responsible for identifying funds to continue the then-mission of educating ministers. The present-day impact of these historical decisions indicates that strategic planning was evident even at the start of colleges in the United States.

The same could be said for two-year colleges. The William Rainey Harper and J. Stanley Brown experiment—known as Joliet College—required forethought. The goal of creating a freshman and sophomore year outside the typical university model had to require strategic planning elements to achieve the goals in enrollment growth and curricular development. Even during the community college boom years (1950–1970), the historical accounts indicate that a college was being added almost on an average of one per week. The leaders involved with gaining the necessary approvals and setting up the institutions were—knowingly or not—involved with strategic planning. Hence, it would not be plausible to argue that Generation X presidents were the first to use strategic planning since the Silent and the early Baby Boomer generations were exclusively at the helm during that period.

This chapter is also not about how Gen X presidents are using a different approach—or for that matter—gaining a different type of result with strategic planning. In fact, a Google search using the words "community, college, strategic, and planning" literally yields millions of results in mere seconds. The links listed on the webpages are connected to strategic plans that vary in length, focus, and goal.

While some of the documents resemble detailed road maps with nested departmental objectives, others are tightly knit sentences or phrases that can fit in a pocket-size trifold. They cover a range of philosophies from a central focus to a dispersed approach. For example, a group of the plans identify important initiatives like equity and inclusion as a stand-alone goal, and others take a position of folding the imperative into all aspects of the plan. So now that there is a clear understanding about what the chapter is "not" about, the question that remains is how do Gen X presidents differ in their approach to strategic planning? The answer is simple—it is not the approach, but rather the context.

Never in the history of community colleges has any generation of leaders had to, not only face, but lead through, the cornucopia of complex concerns that currently exist. As the number of college leaders born between 1965 and 1980 (Fry 2016) begin to assume the chief leadership role at the nation's two-year colleges, the strategic planning processes must take several factors into consideration. Every Gen X president will have to deal with at most all and at the least several of the following topics during a strategic planning process.

MASSIVE RETIREMENT WITHIN INSTITUTIONS

The majority of sitting two-year college presidents would identify themselves as a member of the Baby Boomer generation. A recent American Association of Community College study (Phillippe 2016a, b, c) of nearly 1,000 presidents documents that the median age of respondents was 59. This large group of Baby Boomer leaders—individuals born between 1946 and 1964—has been instrumental in guiding the community college over the past few decades. The same study shared that one-third of sitting presidents planned to retire in five years and 80 percent will retire within ten years.

The presidents are just a portion of the concern as other senior leaders and faculty members follow a similar pattern for those in the same generation. The impending loss of institutional memory and historical context can lead to organizational blind spots that can cause a setback for future presidents. Gen X presidents will have to lead strategic planning efforts that may not be able to build on the nuances of institutional memory unless they can capture that memory before it is lost.

GOVERNMENT EMPHASIS ON
PERFORMANCE FUNDING

According to the National Conference on State Legislature (2015), over thirty-five states have some type of policy focused on the funding of higher education. While this policy direction is recent for many states, the scale of impact will be unknown until future years. A significant percentage of presidents who were in office during the crafting of legislation will be retired by the time the policies are functioning at full scale. This will be a challenge for many remaining Gen X presidents as the shift from being primarily funded by enrollment migrates to the emphasis on completion.

Strategic planning within this realm will cause additional pressure on the institution to become more transparent to a public that may not understand the operational constraints. The very resource colleges need to educate students is the same one being redirected away from the institution if certain metrics are not achieved. This creates a difficult narrative to understand—especially for two-year colleges and open access four-year institutions. The upcoming wave of presidents will be responsible for aiding in the creation of a new narrative either to educate the public on the access-to-success conundrum or facilitate a strategic planning process that rewards employees based on state-styled metrics. Hence, as success increases with student persistence and completion, more resources could be made available as a result of performance increases and scaling opportunities.

THE ACCESS TO SUCCESS PARADIGM SHIFT

For decades the community college has been higher education's symbol of the road forward for a diverse population of students. The growth in the number of community colleges since the 1960s has been a welcomed source of opportunity for millions of students. The states and local communities were supportive as operational funds were traditionally provided based on the number of full-time equivalent students studying during the academic year. During this period college strategic planning efforts were focused on attracting and enrolling more students. The common annual conference lead-off question for most presidents was, "How is enrollment looking?"

It was—and still is to a certain point—a standard to list a college's enrollment trajectory as a part of the institution's website overview and in the president's one-page biography. However, the Achilles heel of the community college was not the inability to attract students; it was the inability to replicate the "success indicators" of four-year institutions. According to NCES (2016) the six-year baccalaureate degree graduation rate for four-year institutions is 60 percent while comparable time of three-year associate degree graduation rates for community colleges is 30 percent. Gen X presidents will inherit the responsibility of creating strategic plans that are designed to emphasize and produce student success.

While this paradigm shift may appear to be a simple task, this effort could be the single most important issue of the Generation X presidency. This group of loners (Gen Xers), many of whom were left home as latchkey kids and who watched how the failure of large institutions and organizations jeopardized the lives and retirements of Baby Boomers, will approach this task from a practical perspective. This characteristic is rooted in the experience of watching sincere promises such as marriage, pensions, and public figures, become undone due to uncontrollable factors.

Generation X takes a different approach focused on investing time and energy into decisions within their sphere of influences. Therefore, instead of spending time discussing the national challenges related to the student success agenda, the Generation X president will focus on his or her college service area/region. The solution may be different depending on the institution and its cultural appetite for change. As this paradigm shift conversation has been a topic within community college circles for a number of years, the plan to aid institutions in the transition will take time to bring strategies to scale.

NEED FOR TECHNOLOGY AND USE OF ANALYTICS

The strategic planning process requires the use of data in various ways. A comprehensive collection of data reports can tell the historical story of where the institution has been providing a reference point of strength and challenge. Present data can aid in the identification of immediate opportunities for partnerships. The forecasting reports will yield insight for the concepts on the horizon and "growth spaces" that may elevate an institution to greatness. The last several years of student success summits have also pointed out the desperate need to be able to model different scenarios and disaggregate the data to get to the root of the problem.

The systems needed to track and predict student success will only become more robust and responsive. While past presidents may have had the need to collect and report data, the Gen X presidents will have to find a way to mine and use the data to drive certain results (Stark 2015). Hence, it is no longer acceptable to know how many students are wearing green shirts. Gen X presidents will be required to articulate the best academic pathway, support services, and engagement opportunities for the students in green shirts to be successful. For many institutions, this approach may not be financially feasible since the cost of these systems will compete against the need to upgrade technology for student-facing needs.

RACE RELATIONS

Our nation has had an intricate history with respect to race relations. While progress has been made over the past decades, recent incidents have caused certain wounds to be exposed. As a result, this intense debate has spread to college campuses across our nation. The Chronicle of Higher Education has published a series of articles that have documented the downfall of senior executives—including college presidents. Many of the "earlier than expected" retirements or resignations have been linked to the failure to appropriately respond to a list of generated student demands.

This is relevant to strategic planning as student-proposed demands—although well intentioned—are not short-term concerns. For example, one reoccurring demand focused on the desire to increase the number of minority faculty members to reflect student body percentages. This appears to be a simple request from one perspective. The work needed to achieve this goal cannot be accomplished in one or even five years. A May 2016 AACC Data Brief *Diversity in Instructional Staff* points out that despite nearly half of the community college student population being identified as a minority, over 75 percent of the faculty are Caucasian. Of the remaining faculty members who are considered minorities, the African American and Hispanic groups represent 7.4 percent and 5.5 percent, respectively.

The approach and planning required to achieve this goal depends on the institution, its location, and the resources it can devote. For a rural two-year college, this could require a significant commitment of resources to include implementing a trailing spouse program and a retention bonus. The Gen X presidents will need to address these types of concerns in a manner that reaches the goal of both the institution and student.

DEMOGRAPHIC SHIFT

There are a number of published articles that posit the nation will become majority minority between 2038 and 2040. In fact, a recent 2015 *U.S. News and World Report* article (Wazwaz) pointed out that based on the 2014 US Census, this is already a fact for children under the age of five. Hence, over the next thirteen years, institutions must lend their attention to strategically preparing for a shift in student demographics. This is relevant as current student success data—in two- and four-year institutions alike—indicate an existing achievement gap between Caucasian, Hispanic, and African American students.

If the achievement gaps persist into the future, and the predicted demographic shift is realized, institutions will experience a decline in persistence and graduation rates. As strategic planning includes an enrollment management outlook, the inability to reach national success goals while sustaining moderate enrollment increases would jeopardize the integrity of any long-range assumptions. Gen X presidents will have to partner with all stakeholders to address the aforementioned observations in a deep and systemic manner.

Many Baby Boomer presidents have started the dialogue and have made noticeable progress by implementing a number of initiatives. Whether Achieving the Dream, Complete College American, Completion by Design, or a similar completion-orientated program, the pending retirement group of presidents have largely led the conversation and benefitted from early observations. Gen X presidents will have to find a way to connect the lessons learned from these early conversations with the new realities that have got to emerge in the future.

PUBLIC–PRIVATE PARTNERSHIPS

The two-year college has been consistent in its desire to be connected to its local community. This aspiration has manifested itself in myriad ways. Whether through a locally elected board, county/city financial support, or business advisory boards, community colleges have identified ways of staying connected to their surrounding area.

Yet, even with the strong linkages, the institutions were able to rely on state funding as a viable source of support. For example, a March 2016 AACC Data Brief *Where the Revenue Comes From* shows during 2008–2009 academic year community colleges received about 36 percent of their support from state resources. Six years later, colleges are reporting that the state support has declined to 30 percent. With the decrease in state support, student tuition has risen to 30 percent of college revenue. Gen X presidents will have to lead strategic planning efforts that forge partnerships with entities outside the institution.

For example, through its Community Partnership for Attainment (CPA), the Lumina Foundation has invited colleges to collaborate with other local entities to generate vision alignment that leads to a stronger talent pool with applicable credentials. The CPA approach recognizes that institutions can benefit from working with other public and private agencies to reach certain benchmarks—including completion. Hence, the future of successful regions will be based on the ability for local partners to set common goals, share resources, and create solutions at a macrolevel. This approach can lead to a synergistic funding approach helping all to benefit without a duplication of effort.

COLLEGE AFFORDABILITY

As mentioned earlier in the chapter, the concept of college revenue mix is a major concern for all presidents. The four-legged stool of tuition, state funding, federal aid, and designated support (i.e., grants, gifts, and so on) is not as stable as in the past. One leg of the stool that is influenced by institutional leaders is tuition. Contrary to the belief of some critics, tuition has never been a way to collect additional revenue at the expense of students, parents, and the federal government. Many institutions depend on tuition as a source of revenue to close the gap in a budget created to support the institutional brand and the specific learning experience a student chooses.

The preceding generations of presidents somewhat benefited from substantial investments from state funding. During this span of time, tuition although increasing due to inflation and similar factors was not a major concern on a broad scale. With the decrease of state support and the increase in expenses due to student expectation, cost of talent expertise, and ongoing infrastructure needs, tuition has been on an incline. This trend caught national attention in 2012 when for the first time college loan debt surpassed credit card debt to become the number one source of financial obligation (Chopra 2013). With an increased level of scrutiny on tution cost, Gen X presidents will have to be prepared to strategically plan for times when tuition increases are limited or not approved.

MOVEMENT TO MONUMENT

Historical documentation and current recollections about the early community college tend to create a picture of innovation and flexibility. As community colleges multiplied rapidly during the 1960s and 1970s, it was not unusual for faculty, staff, and administration to create solutions for complex problems with little debate or fanfare. It was quite normal to "try something different" without going through a lengthy approval process. The mission of the community college was to be different from the traditional four-year model. Instead of being selective and viewed as a gatekeeper, community colleges were open access and viewed as a dream creator.

The traditional four-year institution was primarily focused on research and publishing, and the community colleges were interested in teaching and service to the community. The universities were designed to create and impart knowledge to a smaller segment of the population; the two-year colleges were to create learning opportunities for "whosoever will." The decision to join the community college—or movement—was based on a deep desire to do something different while being comfortable with the unknown.

However, over the last fifty years, the community college has been working to craft an identity narrative that appeals to students, businesses, and communities. The broad approach to serve multiple needs has placed a strain on
resources. For example, colleges once known as nimble incubators of creativity have slowed investment in new programs in an attempt to review the
business case and job outlook. In the past, some institutions would greenlight
the scaling of intriguing ideas without an extensive data collection phase; but
currently, it is routine to hear skeptical colleagues slow down the progress of
an intervention displaying the modern pilot-to-scale killer mindset of "the n
is too small." This begs the question, "When did the Movement turn into the
Monument?"

A significant percentage of those who are in senior leadership group are
preparing for retirement, and that group happened to be the contributing
architects of the community college. The Gen X presidents will be faced with
facilitating the development of strategic plans with a sense of urgency while
seeking to honor the role of a pivotal generation and their contributions.

These nine topics are not intended to represent an exhaustive list of factors that will shape the strategic planning process for Gen X presidents. As
community colleges begin to wade deeper into these complex issues, the
unknowns will begin to emerge and possible solutions discussed. At best, Gen
X presidents will be able to build on the strong foundation developed by the
leaders who have shaped this uniquely American form of higher education.
Yet, if the winds of change are not cooperating, then Gen X presidents will
determine what their legacy will be for the Millennial presidents.

Chapter Eight

Trust and Empowerment

A Declaration of Interdependence

Allen Goben

Generation X leaders tend to more fully engage all levels within an organization to create progress. While Baby Boomers (Boomers) and older generations appear more comfortable working within traditional hierarchies and politics, Gen Xers (Xers) just ignore or sidestep these inconvenient and progress-thwarting aspects of communication and leadership where bureaucracy often outweighs common sense. Trust and empowerment help define a very different Xer approach where all ideas are valid and all people are valued. This chapter will explore such an engagement method called Needs/Goals/Barriers/Solutions (NGBS) and show how it effectively engages all people in multigenerational success.

If you participate in any leadership meeting led by Boomers, the phrase "buy-in" is regularly woven into the conversation. Considering traditional, top-down hierarchical approaches common among colleges, gaining "buy-in" sounds like a good leadership goal. However, while it is often necessary, Xers view buy-in as a lazy way out of true and authentic leadership. Empowering frontline employees as well as administrators to become collaborative solution-creators develops a culture where ownership is more important than buy-in. A culture of empowering ownership is built upon trust, and this is perhaps one of the largest differences in Xer leadership. Xer leaders tend to be naturally trusting toward frontline employees.

Xer culture offers many contradictions. For instance, Xers tend to distrust authority figures but extend considerable trust to the masses of employees. Xers came of age with unprecedented freedom compared to previous generations. Thus, they balk considerably when constrained or inspected by supervisors. They question motives when directives are given without explanation. As leaders, though, Xers are self-effacing and lean toward information culture. They give fewer directives in favor of nonhierarchical problem solving.

It is important to note that Xers do work toward buy-in and especially so when things have to be done in a hurry. Nevertheless, ownership is preferred even though it takes longer and often appears less tidy. The difference is palpable; ownership efforts take longer to create but produce self-sustaining results. Buy-in efforts are deployed more rapidly but then require more monitoring. The "police work" style monitoring is often damaging to an organization, and particularly so when many Xers are present in the workforce.

So how do Xers achieve more ownership and create self-sustaining solutions? The first step is by shedding ego-based power struggles. Xers, typically, are more interested in being successful than in being "right" about something. They have followed Boomers for so many years who cling to the ego of "golden chair" positions in an organization. Thus, they are long accustomed to performing without boosting their own ego by exercising direct power. Xers use more indirect power by coordinating and facilitating inclusion. Thus, Xers find creative ways to engage others in defining issues and creating solutions.

One such approach is called NGBS. It hinges upon allowing employees to offer input on an important topic, such as improving student learning and success at a college. Employees may participate in a survey and follow-up focus groups, broad-scale retreats, and so forth to provide insights into their top needs, goals, barriers, and solution ideas related to improving student learning and success or any other topic of high importance. Qualitative compilation of this input results in major "bucket" areas needing improved focus and an additional list of miscellaneous topics needing support. This nonthreatening way to express issues frames each challenge as an opportunity to succeed. And, it provides a great road map within each "bucket" as detailed input results in tangible action.

Thoughtful progress is made through ad hoc Task Teams formed around everyone's input. This answers the inevitable questions of, "Why are we doing this?" and "What is in it for me?" Since follow-up action is based upon everyone's input, the highest hierarchical level of leaders are justifiably viewed as supportive problem solvers rather than dictatorial managers. Ownership is further enhanced as faculty and staff members are allowed to choose the Task Team efforts they will engage in directly. Leadership Team members, then, do not have to police implementations. Progressive innovation champions emerge at all levels.

Following is an overview of an NGBS survey and corresponding results that drove campus planning at Tarrant County College (TCC) Northeast Campus. This effort began in late 2014 with an NGBS survey administered in early 2015, and it continues to drive campus planning. The NGBS survey had above a 30 percent response rate—about double the usual rate. Initial data were categorized into four "buckets" that were shared at a President's Leadership Retreat involving approximately seventy-five faculty, staff, and administrators in June 2015. Initial results were further analyzed and solidified into four main areas of need:

1. Supporting Student Needs
2. Improving Communication
3. Improving Effectiveness and Efficiency
4. Improving Infrastructure (including Facilities and Technology)

TCC's NE Campus Leadership Team further considered all input and developed Steering Teams for each of the four areas. Task Teams working with each Steering Team were then created to research and implement strategies developed during the retreat. Care was taken to blend faculty, staff, and administrators on all teams as well as to cross-pollinate between departments and divisions, so that all members of the TCC team would continually fuel true collaboration. The following Steering Teams and associated Task Teams were formed:

Student Needs Steering Team

1. Academic Probation Recovery Task Team
2. Assessment of Student Needs Task Team
3. College Transfer Task Team
4. Exemplary Practices Task Team
5. First Time in College Student Engagement Task Team
6. Science/Technology/Engineering/Math Task Team
7. Student Leadership Task Team
8. Student Planning and College Entry Task Team

Communications Steering Team

1. Campus Programs Task Team
2. Campus Updates Task Team
3. Information Station Task Team
4. SharePoint Planning Tool Task Team
5. Stackable Credentials Task Team
6. Student Updates Task Team
7. WIGs-Day Update (Wildly Important Goals) Task Team

Effectiveness and Efficiency Steering Team

1. Effectiveness and Efficiency Task Team
2. Professional Development Task Team
3. Supplemental Instruction Task Team

Infrastructure Steering Team

1. Campus Space Utilization Task Team
2. Community and Industry Education Off-Campus Centers Task Team
3. Infrastructure Needs Task Team
4. IT Support and Training for Student Planning Task Team
5. Social Media and Student Media Task Team
6. Sticky Space Development Task Team
7. Texting Technology Task Team

These teams met over 2015 and 2016, and have been empowered to accomplish tasks working across the campus hierarchical structure by reporting results directly to the Campus Leadership Team. The Leadership Team can then act more promptly and communicate results.

Literally hundreds upon hundreds of ideas were shared via the NGBS survey and in subsequent meetings. While not all ideas can be developed into implementation strategies, it is crucial to honor each idea with genuine consideration. When this is accomplished, people may feel more valued and a part of transformational progress even if it is not exactly as they had envisioned. To truly honor the many contributions, leaders must not only shed ego but also redevelop their view of the organizational hierarchy.

Traditional hierarchies depict a top-down flow of information and decisions. The president, vice presidents, deans, directors, and so forth are shown at or near the top of the chart while frontline faculty and staff are seen at the bottom as seen in Figure 8.1.

Xers simply do not view organizations in this fashion. They are skeptical of traditional authority and suspicious of anyone claiming to have all the "right" answers.

Many Xers envision a flipped version of the usual organizational chart, one where the president and vice presidents are at the bottom supporting more weight instead of at the top controlling subordinates. This places frontline faculty and staff near the top. Faculty and staff, in turn, directly support students as seen in Figure 8.2.

This is not to assert that students then control things from "above" the chart. Rather, it is to postulate that people do not need to be controlled. People need to be supported and engaged as partners in an organization's mission.

So how do Boomers and other generations such as Millennials respond to this Xer approach to leadership? Boomers from most areas and levels appear to respond positively. Engagement and empowerment, in general, seem to be pretty popular. However, Boomers in "power" positions can feel disenfranchised as their roles are redefined to become facilitative supporters instead of authority figures. Many have struggled with a transition away

Figure 8.1   Traditional Organizational Hierarchy.

from the comfort of hierarchical power and time-honored political ways of accomplishing objectives. Once they have adapted, however, Boomer leaders can flourish with experience and political skills to fully engage the breadth of employees in high-reaching collaborative objectives.

Dr. Pamela Fisher, a retired Baby Boomer college president, said that her "... generation set out to overturn the establishment." She went on to reflect that, in order to overturn the establishment, Boomers had to *become the establishment*. This seems a powerful reflection worthy of note to Xers as well as Boomers. If Boomers have become the very thing they set out to disrupt and overturn, then would partnering effectively with Xer leaders and colleagues create the bright and worthy future they once envisioned? Would Boomers and Xers who now hold most significant leadership positions create a future of broad engagement and ultimate progress?

Authors of *Generations* (Strauss and Howe 1991, 80–90) theorized that today's Boomers and Xers are quite similar to Thomas Jefferson's *Idealist (Boomer)* and George Washington's *Reactive (Xer)* generations. The

Figure 8.2   Gen Xer Organizational Concept.

older *Idealist* and next-younger *Reactive* generation leaders mutually supported each other to create great societal progress amidst a crisis. Whereas Jefferson and Washington forwarded an agenda based upon a Declaration of Independence, might today's leaders jointly manifest a *Declaration of Interdependence*?

And what of the Millennials? This generation is rapidly moving into leadership roles as well. Millennials respond very favorably to engagement and empowerment methods such as NGBS. They have expressed appreciation not only for inclusion but also for the framework. Whereas Xers often enjoy a complete lack of framework to rev their creative engines, Millennials seem to like a basic framework within which to operate. The Steering Teams and Task Teams, for instance, offer Millennials a chance to be leaders of important efforts that achieve tangible results. The NGBS approach, then, is helpful and timely for all generational groups.

As we weave a tapestry of collaboration and progress, we must honor great traditions without being beholden to "that's the way things have always been done" concepts. There is an old story about a young man who asks his mother at a family dinner, "Mom, why do you cut both ends off of the roast beef before you put it in the pot and cook it?" His mother tells him that she is not sure, because his grandma just taught her how to cook that way. When his grandma arrives later they ask her about this cooking secret. She responds by saying that, when his mom was a girl learning how to cook, they only had a very small pot for the roast so had to cut the ends off to fit it inside.

Just as it is vital to avoid "that's the way we've always done it" traps, conversely, we must also beware of simply chasing every "shiny new toy" best practice. Just because something is new does not necessarily mean it is better or will work within the context of any organization. People must have time to think, dream, and plan together to determine which innovative ideas have merit and might be implemented or even augmented.

Multigenerational collaboration done right, then, is based upon trust, inclusion, and empowerment. When all ideas are valid for consideration and all people are valued, tangible and collaborative progress occurs naturally as organizational health is supported. The NGBS approach is one way to broadly engage people in healthy conversations, honor great traditions, and focus on innovative progress. Vision for the organization's future and for daily operations is developed together, while many lessons are learned and shared to fuel progress.

Sometimes we find the most profound life lessons in children's books, such as this one from *The Ghost Dance* (McLerran 1995, 21–22) where the author wrote, "If all hold to the dream, the magic will be strong—be strong to call back what we loved the most, and of the new keep what is good, weave old and new in harmony." Perhaps this is the preamble to the *Declaration of Interdependence*.

Chapter Nine

From Latchkey Kid to Latchkey President

Steven R. Gonzales

From another perspective, the completed altered demographic of who attends and works for community colleges since its inception into higher education suggests that it is a new era for community colleges. In one regard, under the Obama Administration community colleges have received long overdue national attention and recognition for the role they play in fulfilling society's higher education and workforce needs. Community colleges are at a historically unique time for a variety of reasons. Changing demographics have great potential to create new challenges and opportunities for college leaders. Of the many demographic characteristics to study, let us focus on the relationship between age and leadership in today's community college.

During no other time have college presidents faced the challenge of leading employees and students from several coexisting generations on their campuses, a condition not likely to change anytime soon. For the Gen X president to be cognizant of the reality that at least five generations either attend class or work on campus can affect his or her success and effectiveness as a leader. Gen X presidents must learn to lead in this new era. Students and employees bring a wide range of common generational traits along with perceptions held of other generations into the classroom and workplace that attribute significantly to the overall culture of the college.

All this sparks the question of how anyone can possibly lead with so many distinct generations on campus. Fortunately, much is written on multigenerational leadership, a term coined to describe the application of leadership to coexisting generations in one organization. While much of the existing research concentrates mostly on the corporate workplace setting, this chapter will focus on multigenerational leadership in community colleges for the Gen X president.

As a Gen X president, you are the bridge between the generational groups. For those colleges that have child-care centers or preschools on campus, it is conceivable that ages may range from several weeks to several decades old! And while employees and students do not have placards hanging from their necks to indicate respective generational membership, perhaps these recognizable behaviors may help. For example, traditional-aged students typically defined as those between the ages of seventeen and twenty-four are considered to be a part of Generation Z. You are likely to recognize them as they whiz by on a skateboard with ear buds on and texting at the same time. It is quite plausible that Gen Zers on campus view you as much too old and too uncool to understand or relate to them.

At the same time, you can find a Baby Boomer behind that print newspaper reading the previous day's history in your campus coffee shop. While the Baby Boomer may not be innocently flaunting their age while on a skateboard, they have other ways to remind you of their age by referring to as *young man* or *lady*, *dear*, *kiddo*, or some other term that essentially translates to, "In case you didn't notice, I'm older than you." Once again, a group on campus may see you as unfit because you are simply too young and too hip to lead their college.

In a recent study, *The Multi-Generational Leadership Study*, 44 percent of Millennials respondents believe they are the most capable generation to lead in the workplace. But when asked which generation is most capable of leading, 51 percent of all respondents feel that Gen Xers are the best choice for the workplace (Staff Reporter 2015). While this may be good news for the Gen X president, it may also suggest that nearly half of the Millennials in your organization possibly view themselves as better suited for your job. Perhaps it is better for your ego to focus on the latter statistic and feel confident that more than half of *all* employees believe you are the prime person for the role because you are a Gen Xer.

Although the corporate workplace is growing accustomed to a recent trend where more Millennials and Gen Xers are leading in corporate organizations, the proportion of Gen X presidents in the community college lags behind their corporate peers. In 1996, approximately 25 percent of presidents were between forty and fifty years of age (Vaughan and Weisman 1998). According to a study conducted in 2012 by AACC, 27 percent were between the ages of thirty-four and fifty-four, mostly Gen Xers (Teckle 2012). The Great Recession is credited for delaying Baby Boomer retirements, thereby tempering the much speculated tsunami of vacant president and other administrative leadership roles in community colleges. Although while some Gen Xers on the upper end of the age scale were ready nearly ten years ago to assume the presidential role, chances are good they had to wait longer or give up on the dream entirely.

Today, Baby Boomers still hold roughly three-fourths of the presidential positions in community colleges. But that is changing quickly. Many indicators suggest that the Great Recession is behind us and that retirement rates are reaching numbers previously predicted to happen a decade ago. This time, however, colleges are experiencing a double whammy because those who waited to retire, coupled with those who have now become eligible during the past eight years, are leaving all at once.

In the past two years alone, 472 of the 1,132 college presidential positions have turned over—that is 42 percent (Smith 2016). Colleges, governing boards, and search firms are scrambling to find ready candidates in a narrow pipeline. Although the number of Millennials have surpassed Gen Xers in the workforce, most are not prepared for the corner office role due to insufficient experience, education, or both. At the same time, the Baby Boomer workforce continues to rapidly dwindle. So, what options do colleges and governing boards have at this point in filling presidential roles? Not necessarily by default but for many other reasons, it will be the Gen Xer who is hired again and again for presidential vacancies. Gen Xers must answer the call. You could be next!

YOU ARE HIRED!

When you are tapped for the role, besides formulating a compelling vision for your college, expectations abound from stakeholders for you to increase enrollment, improve retention, raise more funds than previous years, increase completion rates, and to somehow cope with doing more with less. Suddenly, as a Gen X president, you have gone from *latchkey kid* to *latchkey president*, leading a college without any metaphorical parental supervision and support! It has become even lonelier at the top.

But before you can begin to address any of those common challenges, a college leader must know who is on the team and how to communicate with, inspire, and motivate them. Newly hired leaders must develop a deeper understanding of the various generations coexisting on campus. While leading a college requires common skills necessary regardless of ages of those on campus, several practices exist for the Gen X president to easily employ to ensure that he or she is an effective and successful leader. These practices are low-hanging fruit that are shared as ways to maximize rate of return on investment of your time. The good news is that they do not require you to increase the budget or hire additional staff. It is free, and now you have to do more with less.

PRACTICE

Generational Knowledge

Having a basic understanding of each generation will help you understand the complexities of leading in the multigenerational community college. A recent publication identified three challenges typically associated with coexisting generations in the workplace: communication, negative stereotypes, and cultural expectations (Taylor 2014). As a word of caution, particularly for those colleges with high number of international students and staff, it is important to note that generational differences reflect historical impact from a US perspective and may not apply to those from outside of the country, which further complicates the task.

Communication

Using tools such as social media will help you connect with Gen Z and Millennials on campus, whereas traditional methods such as phone calls, e-mails, and handwritten notes may work well with Baby Boomers. What is considered formal communication for one generation may be considered informal and unintentionally offensive or even a sign of disrespect to others. For example, posting a congratulatory note in 140 characters or less to recognize the good work of a Millennial on social media will be acceptable.

In fact, that employee may proudly repost for his or her friends, coworkers, and family to see and "like" without ever questioning the method of recognition. With a Baby Boomer, however, recognizing the employee may need to be more formal and require a phone call or personal visit with certificate in hand. Knowing those differences, as subtle as they might appear, can positively or negatively affect morale and your standing with those individuals.

Consider preferred methods of generational communication when sharing or gathering information from employees and students. You may find it best to use a variety of methods to communicate the same message over a period of time. Your marketing department most likely does so already in disseminating important college information such as campus closure notifications or service hour changes. Ensuring effective communication and reaching your employees through various methods is labor intensive but pays huge dividends.

Whether you are new to social media or consider yourself an avid user, invest the time to learn about the power and pitfalls of social media for leaders. Not a week goes by that someone in a high-profile position loses his or her job because of a controversial social media post they cannot take back. And do not forget the value of good old fashioned face-to-face communication regardless of which generation is before you.

As a president, you can work with your college to establish guidelines to determine the preferred manner to communicate with one another. At GateWay Community College in Phoenix, Arizona, employees recently underwent an inclusive and collaborative process to develop workplace expectations. In addition to items such as defining work start time, acceptable absence notifications, or workplace attire, employees thought it was critical to create a collegial environment by identifying expectations on how employees communicate with one another. For example, it is expected that an e-mail or phone call be returned within twenty-four hours. It is also expected that face-to-face communication be the preferred method to address potentially hazardous situations where one has an opportunity to clarify or respond to another person's comments. Those expectations help to establish a foundation for healthy communication that apply to all generations on campus.

Negative Stereotypes

Negative stereotypes associated with generations are perhaps more commonly known than those considered to be positive. Gen Xers, for example, are often described as cynical, apathetic, skeptical, and disengaged. Millennials are labeled as nonmotivated, overly tech reliant, and coming off with a sense of entitlement. Baby Boomers are frequently viewed as workaholics, technologically challenged, and overly ambitious (Patterson 2005). As a leader, rather than focusing on those negative stereotypes, concentrate on those considered to be more positive.

Cultural Expectations

Each generation has expectations about how one conducts himself or herself in the workplace. Baby Boomers, for example, tend to believe that one must be in the office before and after the actual workday, a true sign of a hardworking and dedicated employee, whereas Gen Xers are quite content with putting in the number of hours to sufficiently complete the tasks associated with the job. Millennials, on the other hand, look for opportunities to work away from the office when mostly convenient for their social schedule. As a Gen X president, you are best served to create workplace conditions conducive to those varying workplace norms noting that policies may need to be changed to allow for such flexibility. You should also pay careful attention to workplace beliefs when conducting performance appraisals or offering recognition. A Baby Boomer may become quite frustrated with your public recognition of a Millennial who does not seem to put the "time" into his or her job.

The Wise Sage

Perhaps you have heard at least once that you should respect your elders. Keep that advice in mind recognizing that Baby Boomers have been on this planet longer than you. Momentarily ignore the organizational chart. Because life experiences over a growing number of years often equate to wisdom, you likely have several wise sages on your campus who may not necessarily be in leadership roles. Often, these individuals have worked on your campus for years and are generally respected by many. Those individuals can be a great resource for you by providing historical context of many events that have transpired on your campus making it as it is today. A golden find will be one whom you can confide in and run difficult decisions by to get honest feedback and useful guidance. The wise sage may also help avoid any political land-mines not easily recognized by the neophyte Gen X president.

Do not Keep Them Guessing

Are you a situational leader or transformational leader? Does organization as organism best describe the type of organization you are trying to construct? Your responses to those questions and others regarding your leadership style and organizational theory and how they align to your personal philosophy should be widely shared. While sharing your preferred style or theory, be cognizant of the possibility that many on your campus have not studied higher education leadership, which means that you may need to explain what some terms mean. Your employees will appreciate that information, and you may find some who begin to modify interactions with you, which most often leads to quicker decisions and action. Why? Because you have taken the mystery out of the type of leadership you employ.

Earning Respect

Serving as president is not a popularity contest. Before you set foot on campus, there was at least one person who preferred the other candidate during the search process. Do not waste time trying to figure out who fits the bill. Putting it quite bluntly, they do not have to like you but they should respect you. Because respect is generally earned, take great care in your leadership actions in order to earn the highest level of respect from your employees.

While there are many ways to earn one's respect, displaying consistent and authentic behavior will pave the path. Respect is predicated upon trust, the foundational attribute of any relationship, and trust is undergirded by integrity. If a heavy measure of those characteristics makes up your leadership DNA, then you will likely earn the respect of others. You may even be able to turn the tide on those who did not initially favor you. The following practices are surefire ways to earn one's respect as a leader.

1. Be quick to accept the blame and even quicker to deflect any praise.
2. Be consistent and fair in the treatment of those who work with and for you. Preferential treatment or disparagement of others is equally damaging in an organization.

3. Be able to defend every decision or action with your personal philosophy. If you believe student success is at the core of all you do, then you should be able to tie your decision to your student success philosophy.
4. Invest the time and energy to get to know something personal about each one of your employees. Seeing them first as a human being and not just an employee of your organization will garner total respect with political capital as a possible side benefit for future use when you will undoubtedly have to make an unfavorable decision.
5. Realize as soon as possible that you do not have to know all of the answers. Besides this, no one desires to spend much time with a know-it-all. Furthermore, trying to earn respect from Baby Boomers by constantly proving how much you know can actually be a turn off that is very likely to diminish any respect earned by the would-be whippersnapper. Instead, engage Baby Boomers in decision making by truly valuing their input. Even if you do not use whatever information he or she provides, you will often earn the respect of that individual because you gave him or her a voice in the process.

Tortoise or Hare through Change?

The presidency is not a sprint. It is a marathon, so prepare for the long haul in your attempt to make effective and lasting change in your organization. For the multitasking Gen X president, often the organization is not ready to move quite as quickly as you want. Whether new to the role or beyond the honeymoon period, coming to the hard realization that your pace and the organization's pace rarely align can be quite liberating. For one, your stress levels may decrease dramatically.

Consider, as an example, an organization's desire to change how it communicates important information regarding admissions and registration processes to its students. More specifically, the college wishes to embrace technologies that students tend to use such as applications on mobile devices. The average age of community college students suggests that Millennials and Gen Zers make up the largest portion of your student body; yet, you are asking an employee group consisting largely of fellow Gen Xers and Baby Boomers to implement and regularly apply the new technology. In recognizing the differences between generations and your pace versus that of the organization, adopting a proven change model such as Kotter's Eight-Step Change Model may help to alleviate any personal and organization angst and to ensure a positive outcome.

In 1996, Kotter proposed his model in the international best seller *Leading Change* (2012). Much research can be found on the implementation and proven effectiveness of the Kotter model for change. As you explore the model, you will find recommended practices associated designed to assist in each step and help you navigate to the next.

Take a Hike!

Consider a technique to assist you in learning more about employees and the work they do at their stations often referred to as management by walking around. Due to the high demands of your presidential schedule, intentionally schedule time in your calendar to implement this productive practice or otherwise it will not happen. The endless benefits to this practice include an in-person opportunity to recognize employees for their exceptional work on projects or for regularly showing up to serve students with the highest levels of care and service. Baby Boomers are generally most appreciative of the chance to interact with the college president, especially if you inquire about the pictures of their grandchildren on their desk! You can let your Millennial employee know that you posted that picture of them working during a recent student resource fair and then count the minutes before it gets reposted or liked.

Regardless of the generation you interact with during this time, you are giving employees a chance to learn about you. This unfettered method of communication outside of your direct reports yields very interesting and useful information about organizational culture, processes, problems, and opportunities. Of course, following up on whatever is shared will be the metric used by employees to gauge whether you listened to them.

Group Hug

As a final recommended practice for the Gen X president, embrace the multigenerational team. Develop a positive outlook on having such an age-diversified team who brings so many unique experiences with them to the table. Several benefits exist for the organization to gain when a multigenerational team is in place and works well together. Having a multigenerational team can help to attract and retain talented employees of all ages. Additionally, having a multigenerational team reflective of your college's student body aids in the recruitment and retention of those students. Finally, a multigenerational team ensures diversity in its thinking and problem solving. Tap into the collective wisdom and experiences of all ages available to help you become a more effective Generation X president.

Chapter Ten

Crafting a Rewarding Life

Martha M. Ellis

One of the concerns by persons considering a presidency is the all-consuming nature of the community college presidential role. Observing the schedules of presidents along with the cognitive and emotional commitment to the college, current mid-level and senior college leaders are uneasy about taking on the presidential role fearing that personal lives may suffer. The Gen X presidents confirm that the presidential role is an all-consuming and demanding job. How is all consuming defined? All consuming is absorbing and engrossing, completely taking one's attention. All consuming includes immersion as one makes oneself fully involved in the duties, responsibilities, and joys of the presidency. Being all consumed is also riveting, engaging, gripping, and intriguing. What is the reality of all consuming? The position of community college president is 24/7, 365 days a year.

Why does anyone take on such a demanding position? Overwhelmingly these individuals relate that the community college presidency is their passion and more than a job. They have answered the fundamental question of why they chose to become a president at a community college. Here is an example of a statement that expresses this fervor:

> *The presidency is my calling. I have accepted that. The presidency gives me energy and feeds me. I love what I am doing as I am making a difference in peoples' lives and the community, so it is not a job. While it is true that the position is all-consuming, I do not see it as consuming because this position is my calling. I love this work.*

How a person addresses the all-consuming nature of the position is what makes the difference in being successful in both one's personal and professional life. Gen X presidents address the all-consuming nature intentionally and go in with "eyes wide open" regarding the reality of the time and commitment involved with the position. For the CEOs to be effective in their personal and professional lives, they address the consuming role head on and validate it.

- *I knew the presidency was all consuming on the way in as I had prior mentorship on how to work as college president.*
- *Expectations of the presidency match my work style, ethics, and life.*

It is important for a president to comprehend that as CEO one is "always the president." The life of the president is on the public stage in the local community. The president must be presentable and "on" at all times. This concept is true not only for the college, but also for young children and spouses. The time spent with family also requires the president's maximum attention and energy. The presidency touches every fabric of one's being, everywhere one goes, including at home. The presidents interviewed believe embracing the immersion of the presidency enables them to address the complex and continuous demands of the position. These presidents are crafting a rewarding life.

Presidents talk of learning how to manage the complexities of their personal and professional lives and then learning how to do it effectively. It is a constant balancing act between work and family. Balance is defined as that steadiness that each of us strikes between our own enrichment and depletion that is critical to our physical, emotional, and spiritual health (Suchman and Ramamurthy 2014).

Baby Boomers are credited with starting to influence the need to balance life and work. They started taking their vacations and designating some nights and weekends for time with families. The tendency was to segment personal and professional lives. Boomers embraced deferred gratification by saving time, activities, and money for a future time. Gen Xers appreciate the importance of deferred gratification, but want to enjoy today and share the experience with their family and friends. For example, several individuals noted they would rather have more time off than a salary increase or additional annuity.

While the word "balance" may be used by Gen X presidents, their description of their lives is more about integration of family and personal lives with the presidential position. Rather than keeping their personal and professional lives separate, these presidents find ways to interconnect the college, the community, their personal rejuvenation, and their families.

FIRST THINGS FIRST

What became apparent in analyzing the data of the current study is the balance of work and life is driven by personal values and priorities. The leaders clearly articulated the necessity of discovering these values and priorities while preparing to become a president.

Values

Keeping in touch with personal values is a constant challenge to maintain a moral code for both personal and professional lives. Allocating time for reflecting, soul searching, and spirituality provides the foundation for staying on track with a moral compass to be prepared for making the tough decisions. These leaders developed techniques for infusing long-term personal meaning with everyday behaviors. These presidents admonish that once one enters into this important role, a person needs to take care of spiritual side of life.

Gen Xers believe people will be the best presidents if they keep this moral compass intact and values straight. Values-based leadership was a phrase used by many of these presidents to describe their leadership style. Upon further exploration the leaders explained that it is critical to know what values, beliefs, and boundaries are non-negotiable before taking on a presidency. These systems will be tested repeatedly so it is important to remain true to a strong, well-cultivated, inner core. To keep the presidential position in perspective, regular reality checks were encouraged. Several presidents spoke of realizing that the higher one's position in an organization, there is an increased need for humility.

Priorities

Making time for activities that revitalize a person physically, emotionally, spiritually, and intellectually is critical to being a successful president. Wellness and personal renewal were terms used frequently by this generation of presidents. To avoid emotional exhaustion, loss of relationships and dissatisfaction with life that leads to decreased job performance and poor health, all agree of the need to find a way to personally re-energize. They espouse that being greedy and relentless with time is good. To put it bluntly and directly, resource one's personal life like one does the professional life. The leaders talk of self-care including a wellness program of nutrition and exercise. Most report they get little sleep and are constantly juggling. Some examples from those interviewed include:

- *I find ways to take care of myself by playing golf with friends, practicing my guitar and being attuned to my spiritual side.*
- *People know that I go to the gym and read and then come into the office around 9 a.m. or 10 a.m. I work until 7 p.m. or 8 p.m. at night with evening events and other obligations.*

- *Sometimes you have to unplug for a few hours. I spend time with my kids, but I also have work activities that need my participation.*
- *You have to tell people you are available Monday–Friday with only minimal events on the weekend. Weekends are time with my children.*
- *I get up early before my child. I work out and do other things to re-energize myself and then I can spend time with my son before he goes to school and I go to work.*
- *At work, I follow this sequential process to help me balance tasks: Do, Dump, Delegate, and if all else fails, Defer.*
- *Immediacy to tasks is a prominent priority so don't let paint dry before getting something done. Email back right away—answer quickly to have more time for relationships since tasks are done quickly.*

Support of family is important and how that support is demonstrated varies with the individual. All concur a president needs a family that understands and most express their gratitude at having a strong family support structure. The presidents in our study had a diversity of family structures. The families included traditional families, same-sex partners, single, married with no children, and multigenerational extended family. The very diversity in family structure among the presidents was an important finding of this research.

Understanding what this position means for the president's personal life and family is critical to being effective. Some presidents talk of family members helping balance the juggling of life and work. This may include helping with childcare, being confidants, keeping the individual grounded, and often times providing the reminder that the job is not everything in life.

> *When I was in final interviews for the presidency, my wife and I were introduced to the board. The board asked my wife if she was okay with the all-consuming role that I was about to begin. She said she accepted it. Her response made me feel great. She knows my work is my life, and she supports me. I don't talk about work all the time at home and I schedule time off.*

Another president expressed something that may surprise many:

> *It actually helped when I took another presidency and moved away from my extended family. We schedule trips to visit the extended family and spend quality time with them. When we lived close by we tried to juggle those obligations as well as the immediate family obligations.*

This support is a two-way street and these presidents explain how they have to educate their families on the demands of the job, letting everyone in the family know that as soon as the announcement of presidential selection is made, the president becomes a public figure. This implies that the individual and the family need to be ready. Helping significant others understand when criticism or tough times arise they ought not to take it personally or feel that they need to rescue, protect, or defend their loved one who is the president.

Our CEOs articulated that the presidential duties as not something one must do alone. By involving others in a variety of activities, these leaders address the many obligations as well as grow future leaders.

> *I developed co-consumers so I don't become consumed. I assembled a team (not just my cabinet) who take on the all-consuming nature with me. I have 12 or so people who can carry the mission and the vision into the community as well as internal and external constituents. They can give speeches to the Rotary, Lions, and Kiwanis clubs. I nominate them to boards and commissions, so I do not have to be on all of them. They can advocate for the college to elected officials. I trust these people to help me out.*

Two statements of caution from a few presidents:

- *Don't confuse who you are with the job.*
- *The presidency is what you do, not who you are.*

Not all agree and we will discuss this later in the chapter.

WHAT IS INTEGRATION?

When Gen X presidents describe their lives, integration of family and personal lives with the presidential position is articulated. Rather than keeping their personal and professional lives separate, these presidents find ways to interconnect the college, the community, and their families. Emphasizing to everyone they have a fulfilling life outside of the college is imperative. The president intentionally prioritizes and makes time for these priorities assisting the community and college in understanding these priorities. Gen X presidents know their priorities help integrate work and life.

Taking the family to basketball games and other college events allow for the students and community to see them as more than a president. By taking children to events that are family friendly allows the presidents to meet the obligations of the presidential position while having an enjoyable family outing. One president spoke of taking her family to ACCT conference so they could celebrate her child's birthday.

> *I brought my family to ACCT conference so we could celebrate my child's 5th birthday. My only options were to miss his birthday or to bring the family and have a party with the family during the conference.*

Several talked of bringing children to the office.

Sometimes you have to have a picnic in your office.

This integration allows people at the college to find the presidents more approachable.

The presidents also spoke of flexibility and control of their schedules for time with family, working out, and taking vacations. They value the ability to balance work and family because they can control their schedules. If they need to pick up children, they go. Family first mantra is appreciated by most of those presidents we interviewed. They do not feel guilty for this commitment to their families as this behavior provides a role model for other members of the college community that family is important.

- *I work a lot of hours but I have control over my schedule. It may be wild. If I need to pick up my kids, then I go. If I need to attend a school program at 9am, I go.*
- *I make sure to adjust time so my child knows mom is not at work all the time. We have dinners together as much as possible. I can move work schedule around to accommodate this.*
- *I get up at 4 a.m. by choice and I have priorities to save time on tasks. For example, I do not iron the back of my blouses.*
- *As president, you model behavior for employees of college. If a family issue comes up I drop everything and take care of the issue. This creates a healthy culture for the organization. [You] Model behavior: if you are sick—go home. If your baby is sick—go home.*

Multitasking is a natural part of life. If attending a basketball game, they utilize the time and event for fundraising and relationship building. If they need to participate in community events to represent the college and their children can participate, they include them, for example, riding in parades or participating in volunteer days. Additionally these presidents are tech savvy and communicate through e-mail and social media like Facebook. They fully believe they do not have to be around in person all the time. They also talk of getting lots of work done on mobile devices while doing other activities away from the campus.

Gen X presidents are entering the "sandwich generation: where they are faced with taking care of aging parents as well as children." While this was not a topic discussed in great detail, the issue was emerging. They want to be able to provide caregiving to elders as well as dependent children. One president talked of blogging about the death of a parent and another about sharing the agony of a parent's terminal illness.

This integration does not mean that the family is totally involved in the presidential work or fair game for criticism. The president must draw boundaries for personal life and communicate the limits to the college, community, and the family. As one president noted, "I let the board know when I was hired that my significant other would not be participating in college events or activities." These boundaries and priorities provided the foundation for the underlying first rule of being a president: find the right fit.

It Is All About the "Fit"

The mantra of the right fit is talked about in every conversation about becoming a college president. Virtually everyone who makes it to the final round of interviews is qualified to be a college president. Who is selected and who accepts the offer at a particular college is more about the right "fit" at this time for the college and the finalist. According to Gen X presidents, the fit is also about the integration of the personal and professional life. It is important that institutional mission and values reflect the values of the president and the president's family. It is imperative to think about the college size, location, multi- or single campus, faculty, tenure, unions.

Consider the local elected officials, state policies, legislators, and governance structure. However, fit is also about the community. Is there a church to attend, appropriate food, activities for the desired lifestyle, and preferred education and environment for children? It is important for the president's personal as well as professional life to know the college and community as children and significant others are impacted by this decision. Is this college a fit for them? Several presidents express aspects of decision making and fit.

Why a campus presidency is best:

I have a family with two children. The campus presidency occupies a lot of my time but it is still a good fit for me. It would be hard to manage a chancellor's position with young children. Chancellors work with legislators and elected officials and that is more time consuming with events and situations where you cannot take children. Also chancellors have considerably more travel.

Deciding to stay in a current presidency:

I was recently recruited for another presidency. It is not a good time to leave my current college because of the work we are doing. It is also not a good time to leave because of my family. Where I am now—I got to see my son hit his first home run. You see, it is a good fit for us because my family is part of this community and the college. I declined the invitation.

The first year of the presidency is around the clock due to learning about the college and community culture as well as building relationships. During this year, the president starts to learn the priorities of where to spend time. Understanding what is the right amount of time and type of interaction with the Board of Trustees, the community, and being visible on campus is a delicate balance in and of itself. These are hard lessons learned.

Time requirements differ greatly depending on the nature of the institution and the culture of the community. Is it customary for the president to entertain at home or at a local country club? Entertaining at home may require purchasing a different type of home, different requirements for the family, and a willingness to share private spaces with the college and community. The local county club requires membership and who pays for that membership. What about the perception or actuality of club membership criteria that may be at odds with an equity agenda of the college and/or a personal value?

While no checklist can detail all the factors to consider in determining the right presidency, these presidents clearly articulate that fit is inclusive of the right institution at the right time for where a person is in his/her professional and personal life.

AND YET IT IS A STRUGGLE

The confidence and abilities of this generation of presidents in approaching the all-consuming nature of the position are reassuring. Without the ability to have a work/life balance, these individuals will not be able to continue in these challenging, demanding jobs. As with all qualitative research, the emerging themes arise but with a divergence of how these themes are individualized. Seeing the inconsistencies within interviews as well between interviewees illustrated the complexity of talented and committed leaders trying to "do it all." In one breath, they state that the presidency is what they do and not who they are. In the next breath they explain that the position impacts every fabric of their being-everywhere they go, even when they are at home.

Some Gen X presidents honestly admit the presidency is who they are. They state that they cannot separate the position from who they are as individuals because of the passion and commitment they have toward the college, the students, and the community. In their own words:

- *Work does not have to be all consuming as it is not what I do but who I am.*
- *I cannot tell you when I turn it off. The job becomes part of you.*

Some admit they have no balance in their lives.

- *There are presidents out there who can turn it off. I can't. I take my phone on vacation. My husband says I am married to my cell phone. I am always connected.*
- *I try to take notice of my time. I do not do work/life balance well. I do not know how people do this job with children. I barely have time to take care of the dog. I am so energized and revitalized by the work. I can't think of something I would rather do to enrich my life. (Although, I do play golf.)*
- *The college CEO is an all-consuming position and I have no balance. That being said, my work ethic has not changed. Working long hours has always been my usual when I was a dean and a VP. Sometimes my wife texts me to come home. She worked in higher education so she understands.*

SUMMARY

The presidents in this study clearly understand the all-consuming requirement to be an effective community college president. They embrace this as a fact of the position and intentionally formulate strategies for a satisfying professional and personal life. They do not seek to deny any one part of their lives but rather to balance and integrate professional and personal lives with well-defined values and priorities. All the leaders admit it is difficult to balance children, single parenting, same-sex partners, and/or aging parents. The commitment to the work of the community college president is worth the struggle as they are passionate about what they do each and every day.

Most of these leaders admit it is nice to be a Gen Xer. They have learned much from Baby Boomer mentors both formally and informally on what to do and not to do to have a successful personal and professional life. The female presidents are glad they do not have to worry about having to prove themselves in a man's world. What once were considered alternative personal life styles are now more readily accepted by Boards of Trustees and communities allowing for the openness to interconnect personal and professional lives as defined by the individual president. The journey of the Gen X community college president includes observed, experiential, and learned proficiencies, which enable the individual to intentionally craft a rewarding life.

Chapter Eleven

Crafting a Rewarding Life

A President's Perspective

Stefani Gray Hicswa

By integrating the personal and professional aspects of life, a president can intentionally craft a rewarding life, take risks, and set sights on having a happy family and a fulfilling career. You are able to do it all—just not all at the same time.

TIMING

Climbing a traditional career ladder is not essential, nor is waiting until children are grown to pursue a presidency. Stopping out of your career to have children will not hold you back. Instill the importance of family in campus culture by being genuine and authentic. Do not worry about being the perfect spouse or parent. Invest in a good relationship with your partner and ask others for help. By setting priorities and deciding early on that you will not be all things to all people, you can navigate your life on your own terms. This will give you the confidence to make life-decisions that may even catapult your career.

A CALLING

The college presidency can be all-consuming if you allow it to be. However, if serving community college students is your calling, then you will have the inherent drive to do this work. Create the life you want by working hard, playing hard, setting boundaries, and prioritizing. It helps if you are an adrenaline junkie who needs challenges at this level. Substance is what makes life rewarding.

I do everything with intensity—work, relationships, and vacations. I never ques-
tioned whether my personal life would suffer.

JUGGLING PERSONAL AND PROFESSIONAL LIFE

Drive, together with focus, contributes to success. When you are with your
family, focus on what you are doing whether it is playing hide-and-seek,
backpacking, or working in the yard. When you are at work, shift into high
gear and crank out what needs done. When you get home, let work go so that
you can focus on family. Then get up and do it all over again.

> *When I am speeding down a mountain bike trail, it is hard to think about college*
> *policy revisions, budget cuts, or legislative agendas.*

Challenging physical activities, outdoor recreation, and other hobbies can
help you decompress and truly get a break from the job. The problem with
integrating personal and professional life is that you do not completely check-
out as often as you probably should. Although it takes a lot of effort to juggle
everyone's schedules, you can make it work. Not only will you have lots of
fun in the process, you will find that you are also able to thrive.

PRIORITIES

In mentoring mid- and senior-level community college leaders, they worry
that their personal lives may suffer if they seek a presidency. You do not let
your personal life suffer—you integrate it by setting priorities. Time is a precious commodity, so prioritize carefully and set clear boundaries.

Do not apologize for your priorities or compromise your values for a presidency. You must make choices and set boundaries based on the value you
place on quality time with your family.

> *I have yet to miss a birthday, although I missed a meeting with the Governor to*
> *attend my son's fourth-grade project presentation. The next time the Governor*
> *was in town, I made sure I was there to greet him.*

Make no apologies for bringing kids to the office or to events. They come
with the presidential package.

> *One of my first fundraisers as president at my current college was on an evening*
> *when my husband was unable to make it home on time. My kids changed into*
> *nice clothes and attended with me. They were quite charming and knew every-*
> *one's name before the evening was over. My sons are old enough now that they*

will work the room at events telling potential donors about college initiatives in ways I never could. My family is truly an integral part of the college community.

VIRTUAL PARENTING

An advantageous benefit of a presidency is flexibility. As long as you plan far enough ahead, you can sign-up for field trips and attend children's concerts and school functions. Yet, schedule conflicts cannot always be avoided. There are always functions that compete for your time and attendance.

Due to an important college event, I missed an art show where both my sons' artwork was displayed. As soon as the college function was over, I drove to the show. Luckily, we live in a small town where everything is within five minutes from the college. My family had since left the show, but I still had ten minutes before the gallery closed. I walked-in and FaceTimed my oldest son from my cell phone. He directed me to their art displays one-by-one. Even though I did not have time to go home and get them, I was able to experience the art show with my children, albeit virtually.

Technology, such as FaceTime, can become quality time with your family when you travel. It is so much better to see family members' faces than talk to them on the telephone. From afar, you are able to help with homework, see a gap where a tooth used to be, and help pick out appropriate clothing for school pictures.

We have even employed FaceTime for emergency birthday gifts. "Mom, I need a gift for a birthday party."
"When is the party?"
"Tonight."
"Seriously? What do you want me to get?"
"FaceTime me from the store and I will show you."
Problem solved. FaceTime to the rescue, again.

Perhaps you watched the *Jetsons* cartoons as a child and imagined the overall coolness of video telephones, but did you ever imagine video parenting? It works.

A GOOD PARTNERSHIP

A spouse or partner can be invaluable in integrating you into family activities when you are unable to be there in person. Technology provides a medium to keep you in the loop when you miss family events.

The role of a spouse or partner is an important component of successful work–life integration. Helping to keep you well-grounded through the complex and hectic nature of a presidency is invaluable.

When I do something dumb such as put the salt and pepper in the refrigerator, it is not uncommon for my husband to say, "Way to go, doc." He is good to give me perspective and makes me laugh at the challenges that life throws us.

Nonetheless, a partner must have interests and goals of his or her own. It is important to be appreciative and respectful of your partner's ambitions and disposition, especially if he or she has put a career on the backburner. Invariably personal pursuits will make your partner unavailable to attend all functions with you. Establish good lines of communication and be open about what college events your partner must attend, might attend, and does not need to attend.

If there is a college event that my spouse should attend, I am obligated to say so rather than be mad and pout because he is not being supportive of my career. He knows that an annual black tie fundraiser for a local charity is one of the events that he is "supposed to want to" attend. We make it a date night and have a great time.

ASKING FOR HELP

Just as a president needs to learn to communicate more clearly with a spouse or partner, a president also needs to ask for help. Delegate as much as possible. Just because you *can* do something, does not mean you *should* do it or that it is the best use of your time. For example, even though you have the ability to change the printer cartridge in the office, it is more appropriate to ask for help. In the time it would take to install a new cartridge, a president could have made a fund-raising call or followed up on a budget issue. The same goes for duties at home.

- *One of the best investments I have ever made is hiring a housekeeper. Rather than spending time every weekend cleaning my house, I spend that time with my family.*
- *I also take shortcuts. I do not iron the back of my blouses—they just get wrinkled anyway. More often than not, my bed does not get made nor does laundry get folded. Although I do not maintain my mom's housekeeping standards, by allowing myself these "indulgences" rather than beating myself up, my life is much better.*

Balance is about reconciling expectations and deciding which expectations and standards are negotiable and which are not. With a president's hectic schedule, you also need to take care of yourself and eat well to have the energy you need.

I still maintain my mom's standards regarding the importance of eating home-cooked meals together around the dining room table. I usually eat yogurt and fruit around 4:00 a.m. and make a hot breakfast for my family and me at 7:00 a.m. Most days we eat breakfast and dinner together.

Be creative with other working parents. Think about starting a weekly supper swap with other families in your neighborhood.

On Sundays, I make dinner for three families. They do the same with meals for the other nights of the week. With occasional leftovers and travel, most weekday dinners are covered.

By allowing others to make dinner for your family and hiring someone to clean the house, you are able to free precious time for other priorities. Although it may be harder to ask for help with your children, remember that it really does take a village to raise a child. Friends and neighbors can pick up kids from school and take them to sports practices. Your children may need to spend the night with their friends on occasions when evening events run late.

When a person envisions being a community college president, somehow cleaning vomit while on a conference call with trustees does not come to mind but it happens. Stay true to your values and be flexible.

Invariably, when my husband is out of town, one of my kids gets sick. I have held meetings with a sleeping child on the floor of my office and have worked from home on occasions, including board meetings, when I needed to be with sick kids.

Women presidents in the previous generations pioneered these obstacles. There are countless stories of women who waited to pursue presidencies until their children were grown because they were afraid of being fired if they missed a trustee meeting to be home with a sick child.

I feel quite fortunate to have worked with wonderful trustees who have supported me and my family. I negotiated family travel into my contract for my first presidency, as my sons were 19 months and two months old when I was hired. My board chair, a man in his 70s, did not hesitate in his approval. I made such a bold request not only due to my values, but also because I wanted my new board chair to know that my family is a priority. Although risky, this approach has served me well throughout my career.

CAMPUS CULTURE

Early on, figure out what was best for you and your family. This will let you take risks and make intentional decisions for your life. Do not feel guilty for the commitment you make to your family. This behavior provides a role model to college employees that family is important. If the president can leave work to attend a school program, they have permission to do the same. This creates a healthy culture for the organization.

A positive connection can be made with the campus community through employees' children as well. You are seen as a regular parent at school activities and sporting events.

> *Employees' kids call me by my first name and treat me like any other mom. Sometimes, they stop by my office to say "hi" when they are on campus for an event or summer camp.*

If entertaining in a president's home fits with the culture of the college and community, employees and their children may become frequent guests at your home. Hosting events for new employees and retirees, booster club dinners, and other fundraisers are examples of events that work well with families.

> *We host the athletic teams and other student clubs for various occasions throughout the year. In fact, we host events at our home so frequently that that my sons have begun to make special requests of the caterer for their favorite menu items.*

Be cognizant that since your preferences can be attributed to your "Gen X-ness" you may need to match the preferences of trustees and employees from different generations. This provides a satisfying campus culture for them as well. For example, a board chair may prefer telephonic and face-to-face communication. Sometimes e-mail communication may be required, but know that members of the Silent Generation and Baby Boomers may value in-person communication.

Many Millennial faculty prefer communicating via social media. They are connecting with students in ways other generations could not have imagined. This encourages a president to look at changes such as faculty office hour requirements for example. A president may also want to use a blog or other social media to influence the campus culture in positive ways. Blog about what is happening on campus, decisions that were made, hobbies, and so on. Gen X presidents are generally seen as human and approachable by the campus community and social media enhances opportunities for connections.

AUTHENTICITY AND INFORMALITY

In addition to creating a healthy campus culture, being approachable creates an inclusive environment where people see the president as genuine and authentic.

I find as I grow more comfortable leading from my Generation X preferences, I am dressing down: trading in suits for dress pants and jackets, wearing jeans to basketball games, and stopping by campus on travel days dressed very casually. In the rural community where I live, I find my informality also makes me more approachable. When I go to the grocery store in shorts and a t-shirt on a Saturday, people approach me who may not have otherwise.

CONCLUSION

Whether it is what you wear or how you make decisions, do not worry about following a conventional path. Rather than focusing on climbing a traditional career ladder, focus on being authentic and intentional about the life you want. By being strategic about what you want to experience in life, you seize opportunities to make things happen. Sometimes you have to break the rules to lead the life you want.

I did not think about doing things differently because I was a Gen Xer, instead I set my sights on having a happy family and a fulfilling career.

A president cannot be all things to all people. You have to be intentional about asking for help to create a life where your career as a college president is not all-consuming. Be fiercely committed to both your job and your family. By integrating the personal and professional aspects of your life, you set priorities and know where you will not compromise. While you may not find work-life balance, sometimes the best adventures are when you feel a little off-balance.

All of this makes for a very rewarding life—one that you can craft intentionally.

Being a Mother and a President
Stefani Gray Hicswa

In 2006, I became one of the first-generation X community college presidents in the United States. I did not think about doing things differently because I was a Gen Xer. Instead, I did what felt right for the culture of the college, and for me as a leader. While I have yet to find work-life balance, I have figured out how to navigate the all-consuming nature of the job to craft a rewarding life. Although it has been a wild ride, these have been the best years of my life. I attribute this incredibly enjoyable journey to not always playing by the rules and assimilating various facets of my life.

Pathway to the Presidency

Almost 20 years ago, the president at the college where I worked recruited me for the National Institute for Leadership Development (NILD). During one of the sessions, we were asked to think of the worst college president we knew and consider if we could do better. I had served on a national board of directors and was president of a regional professional association. I had completed my master's degree and was considering doctoral programs. I was in my late 20s, full of myself, and felt bulletproof—of course I could do better.

Upon imprinting that goal, the retreat facilitators asked us to contemplate colleges where we could see ourselves serving as presidents. I chose Miles Community College in Miles City, Montana, and Northwest College in Powell, Wyoming. I selected these colleges because they were in small, rural communities in the western United States with cultures that fit the lifestyle my husband and I desired. During that week, I set intentions that not only shaped my career, but also shaped my life. Today, I am the president of Northwest College, after serving seven years as president of Miles Community College.

Mother and President

Following the completion of my doctorate, I made the difficult decision to deliberately stop-out of my career to have children. Since I had quit my job to pursue a PhD, my husband and I decided to run a ranch in Montana after living apart for two years. Growing up on a ranch, I never thought I would want to go back to that lifestyle; yet, this was the perfect opportunity for us to evaluate our priorities as a couple, examine our goals, and figure out our next steps.

I waited to apply for a presidency until after my second child was born. When I interviewed for my first presidency, my youngest son was two months old and I was 37. Although I was prepared for the interview, I was not prepared to interview with a newborn. I had a new briefcase, shined shoes, and copies of my vitae. However, I did not have a breast pump, bouncy seat, or babysitter. Nevertheless, I got the job and started a few months later. My mother-in-law could not conceptualize how we were going to do it all. She even suggested my husband and sons move in with her so she could take care of them. She lives 2,500 miles away.

When I first became a president, after putting my kids to bed, I went to my home office and caught-up on matters of the day. Yet, most nights, I was up until 3:00 a.m. or so. I quickly realized the time I spent winding my children down in the evening was time that I was able to relax and let the detritus of the day go.

By changing my priorities, I began going to bed shortly after my kids went down for the night. Since I was typically asleep by 8:00 p.m., by 2:00 a.m., I was wide awake. I do not require much sleep, but more than that, I enjoyed the quiet time. I used it to reflect, plan for my day, and of course reply to the never-ending email deluge. I continue this habit to this day. Although as my children get older and their bedtime is later, I find that I usually sleep-in until 4:00 a.m.

When my boys were young, if I was unable to be home in time for dinner, I prioritized my schedule to be home in time to give them baths and kiss them goodnight. Our bedtime ritual, which even to this day includes reading to them, was something

I looked forward to as much as they did. Frequently, I excuse myself from evening events by saying, "I am going home so I can see my kids today."

There is no better icebreaker than showing up for work with baby spit-up on your shoulder.

This job is too hard to worry about being "presidential"; therefore, I am authentically myself every day. When asked about how my family impacts my leadership style, my answer is that it helps me lead with authenticity—because I do not have time to be anything else. College employees have seen me tired, sad, frustrated, ecstatic, and silly. I am totally me and I am not afraid to show it. I have no regrets about how I have done it, nor do I feel guilty. My life is quite satisfying on all levels.

Chapter Twelve

Preparing for the Presidency

What They Did Not Teach You in Graduate School

Martha M. Ellis

There is not one road map to the presidency. There is no one perfect way to prepare for the presidency. Gen X presidents believe that more attention needs to be paid to the preparation of new leaders based on the current and future needs of community colleges. According to those interviewed, there is not a path for future presidents based on where we have been in the past. These leaders firmly believe that sitting presidents and the higher education field have a responsibility to prepare and encourage talented people to move into senior leadership positions at community colleges. Filling the leadership void is a shared obligation between an individual and the higher education writ large.

This chapter begins with the charge to the overall domain of higher education. The field must be more proactive in addressing the current and future vacancies in leadership positions. The next section of the chapter delineates the top ten areas Gen X presidents believe are most needed, and often not taught, to be successful as today's community college president.

WHAT THE FIELD NEEDS TO DO TO HELP GENERATION X AND MILLENNIALS BECOME CEOS INTRUSIVE MENTORING

Chapter 5 of this book discussed how intrusive mentoring was a major component for Gen X presidents to become and stay community college presidents. These presidents repeatedly expressed the desire and responsibility to provide intrusive mentoring for up and coming leaders. They encourage other leaders to do the same. The intrusive approach includes reaching out to potential leaders and providing opportunities for skill development.

95

Presidents need to identify the top rock stars and provide opportunities for leadership

Mentors have to protect young leaders. One president relayed:

Before I was a president, I shared an idea with older colleagues. I thought my idea was great. But the vice president responded to me by saying, "What do you know? You are a young whipper snapper!" That shut me down and I started to doubt my abilities.

The interviewees believe sitting presidents have an obligation to help bridge the changing of generations. While Gen Xers are independent and cynical they are steadfast in believing they have a civil obligation in bringing and valuing multiple generations for the future of community colleges and their communities.

More conversations are needed at colleges to encourage people to be vice presidents and presidents. Succession planning is not prevalent at most community colleges so the pipeline for grooming people for all types of leadership positions is noticeably absent (Ellis, 2012). A way to begin this process is to ask employees about professional goals and how can we help them accomplish these goals? Senior leadership needs to create opportunities for young leaders who are the future rock stars. Through intrusive mentoring presidents should say "You are ready."

Throughout the topics discussed in this book, a resounding theme has been that the president cannot accomplish all the duties of the position single handedly. One supplementary approach to accomplishing the divergent and countless tasks is to include future leaders in the cadre.

1. Nominate these rock stars to local boards.
2. Take these potential senior leaders along in meetings with elected officials, donors, and business leaders. As they acquire the skills, allow them to take the lead in areas of this work.
3. Provide encouragement and support as they grow, develop, and fill their leadership tool box. Explore the areas to help them increase their knowledge base.
4. Help them identify the warning signs that tough times are brewing and tips on how to get through these.
5. Facilitate faculty and staff in leading where they are. Provide opportunities for individuals to reach outside traditional roles to take on diverse leadership opportunities.
   Institutions must be willing to take risks on individuals allowing them to take on leadership roles.

All Gen X presidents talked of people who provided these opportunities for them and they believe it is the responsibility of all presidents to do the same for the younger generations.

Additionally, the larger landscape of state and national community college organizations need to create programs that connect promising senior leaders with a successful president in a meaningful learning experience. More structured networking opportunities at conferences for presidents to meet with people wanting to becoming a president would be advantageous in breaking into the community college "in" crowd. The silent generation presidents are good mentors but they see everything in black and white. Baby Boomers are easy to work with as they have collective idealism but hard to work with because of staunch resistance. Gen Xers respect the Boomers' experience and political savvy stating that it is hard to follow the Boomers. While they appreciate information and wisdom from previous generations, they believe new problems need new leaders.

The Silent Generation and Baby Boomers need to acknowledge that context is different. A president can no longer fly by the seat of your pants due to complexity. GenXers understand why it is different.

Conferences

As mentioned at the beginning of this book, the impetus for this research was two different generational sessions at AACC in 2015. During the last two AACC annual convention and League for Innovation's Innovation Conference, sessions were held featuring Gen X presidents. Each time the room was filled to capacity. This evidence supports the assertion made by the presidents interviewed for this study that more niche sessions are needed for younger leaders.

I have gone to conferences for 15 years and it is all the same people speaking. We need to have new faces. I really do not care how the giants did it. I want to know how current and new leaders are resolving new problems.

Future presidents need more exposure to presidents including sitting and younger presidents, not just the presidents at the end of their careers or retired. People want to see people who look like themselves in the presidential role and are successful. If Gen Xers see Gen Xers then it is easier to recruit for leadership positions.

An enhancement suggested for the ACCT annual conference is the inclusion of more Gen X presidents in presentations and panels. While boards realize presidents do not have to come out of academic backgrounds, they are often not willing to take a risk on a younger person. There is frustration with the current search processes. Sometimes younger candidates barely get a first interview because they have no legacy on paper. A generational gap of ideas may emerge between a president and the board. This becomes evident when recruiting the next generation of community college leaders with the current screening and search process.

> *Pools of candidates never match up with what previous generations want in a current president.*

The values are different between the generations. For example, Gen Xers want to have flexible schedules even as they work long hours. People in their seventies may be more scheduled. Board members might expect a president to be physically present at every event and meeting but the younger generation is comfortable with participating remotely via technology. A scan of businesses outside of academia reveals younger generations move into senior leadership positions more quickly. A bias appears to be prevalent by some boards of community colleges to take a risk on hiring Gen X and Millennials. Boards and search consultants need to start taking more risks on hires from younger generations.

Education

Gen X presidents stress the need for a political will to teach people about higher education. They crave more colleagues with experience and talent on their leadership teams including chief financial officers, chief student services offices, chief information officers, and chief academic officers. Universities have shut down programs and are not picking up the mantle. The professional membership organizations of community colleges are seeking to address the dearth of education. Aspen Presidential Fellows, League for Innovation Executive Leadership Institute, AACC Roueche Future Leaders and Future Presidents Institutes, Kaleidoscope, and National Council on Black American Affairs Leadership Development Institute are examples of the significant programs to address leadership training. That being said, Gen Xers express the desire for revision in these programs. Recrafting competencies around Gen X and new challenges is a necessity for future leaders' success.

> *When I look at the list of speakers at these institutes, it is all the same people. Many times these institutes do not provide substantive information on today's issues. They do help with networking and that is important.*

An added worry about these institutes is the follow-through after the end of the institute. What happens when the participants go back to their institutions?

Who follows up? Who do they call if they have a problem implementing something they learned during the institute?

Finally, a national conversation or summit about the issue of Gen X and Millennials filling the leadership vacuum was proposed. Concomitant with the national conversation would be a national campaign for leadership describing the rewards of leading in a community college to counterbalance the continual dialog of complex challenges and long hours. Underlying this recommendation was the stipulation that Gen Xers are included in the conversation about community colleges and preparation of future presidents.

> *Look at the list for participants in Reclaiming the American Dream. How many GenXers do you see on that list? GenXers want to be at the table.*

The Top Ten: What a Person Needs to Know to be a President Today

Presidents of all generations agree there is a huge learning curve as a person begins the presidential position. The knowledge required to be a president requires much deeper learning than leadership theory. The Gen X presidents provided topics they believe are essential to be successful in the community college presidency today. The top ten recommended themes include:

1. Find a mentor
2. Build skills
3. Build relationships
4. Know finance
5. Acquire fund-raising abilities
6. Learn to navigate politics and advocate
7. Engage faculty and staff
8. Know appropriate uses of technology
9. Develop board relations
10. Become proficient in identified little things.

1. Find a Mentor

To recap previous perspectives, mentors played a significant role in Gen X presidents' road to the presidency and they believe every leader needs at least one mentor. These presidents feel a responsibility to be mentors to the next group of presidents. The responsibility, however, also rests with the aspirant leader to reach out to leaders and ask admired leaders to become mentors. It is incumbent upon the rising rock star to seize the opportunities provided by sitting presidents.

A mentor can explain to an aspiring leader how he or she can do this job with kids, same-sex partners, and other family obligations while being true to one's values. Spend time with a president to learn the inside view of the presidency. Direct observation of a president affords a person a glimpse into the good, the bad, and the ugly and how a person might lead similarly and differently.

> *I shadowed a president and learned that everywhere she went she represented the college and was always the president. I could bring up questions about her approach and talk through the process of her decision-making.*

People tend to underrate the importance of a network. Developing a strong network with colleagues of all generations is indispensable to securing and thriving in a presidency. Have conversations with peers of same generation. Have conversations with leaders from older and younger generations.

Numerous leaders admit they do not have to have all the answers. They reach out to mentors and their network to ask for advice and guidance. Every leader needs someone to call upon. Someone to be a cheerleader and confidant. Someone to really connect with. Mentors are not just college presidents. Mentors can be leaders in different professions. Some mentors are across the country and some next door. They are different ages, genders, and ethnicities and have different fields of expertise. The essential element of a quality mentorship is ensuring the moral compass of the president matches with the trusted confidant and mentor.

2. Build Skills

The presidency is hard work, so seeking opportunities to help strengthen leadership skills are worth it. Achieving success takes planning, time, and hard work. The degree gets a person in the door but does not guarantee the skills to do an effective job.

Aspiring leads are encouraged to take on leadership opportunities in areas outside of current positions and raise their hands to get a taste of the many facets of presidential work.

> *Raise your hand and say I want to do this. Seize and build on opportunities.*

One way to explore and test administrative skills is undertaking interim positions. Interim positions afford exposure to different people and departments in the college. If possible, a promising leader should try on roles to understand effectual strategies with Board of Trustees and with faculty organizations. Until a person walks in administrative roles he or she will not understand how these positions will change a life.

The job is not for everyone. The daily responsibilities take inner strength and resolve. If a person does not like seeking opportunities, asking for resources and creating innovative solutions, then this is not the right job. A person needs to be comfortable with knowing that the job is never complete. Sometimes projects are never-ending because they continue to evolve. A president is constantly pulled in many different directions. This job is not for people who like structure.

Reviewing AACC and Aspen competencies to validate that these skills resonate with a person and future career activities can be insightful. A relatively quick way to bolster skills is participating in programs to prepare for the presidency such as those discussed earlier in this chapter. Talking to search consultants who write presidential profiles offers awareness of skills hiring committees deem necessary for leadership in the twenty-first century.

> *Get engaged, reach out to people, search consultants, and talk to presidents.*

Read everything and pay attention to research to stay abreast of the fast-changing environment in community colleges. Change is the hallmark of the landscape in higher education.

- *Execution of major change is the next big skill needed by presidents.*
- *Learn how to set the tone of the college, who is really calling the shots.*

The complexity and multiplicity of challenges facing community colleges today require leaders to look outside their colleges for innovative solutions.

> *Know how to form partnerships as this is the academic reality now.*

Finally, never forget to hone the basic skills.

- *Learn how to manage policy, resource allocation, and hiring good personnel.*
- *Five things I wish I had known about when I started—finances, facilities, academics, working with a board, and politics.*

3. Build Relationships. It Is About People

All the presidents stressed that the job is all about working with people and building relationships with a wide variety of stakeholders. While the president may not always agree with every stakeholder and often times must tell people "no," the president must do so with diplomacy and tact.

- *You must have a tangible focus on how to interact and survive in politics of previous generations.*

- *Learn how do you maneuver within and how you bring about change effectively.*

Enjoying being around people is an advantageous attribute for a president.

Those interviewed suggest a person cannot have the personality that one person can do the job independently. Relationships are necessary to getting the job done; not just getting the job. Delegation is paramount as no person can do this job alone. Pick up the phone, twitter, or e-mail to engage people.

- *You really must like being around people and working with a wide, diverse group of people.*
- *Who do you know to get the presidential position? Who do you know inside and outside the college to drive the mission? The second question was a surprise.*

The presidents articulated cranking out tasks as quickly as possible to be able to focus time and energy on relationships. Leaders stressed not to fear caring about people. Interact with people on the most basic level realizing the president cannot be all things to all people.

- *I spend as much time as I can with students; we are engaged on a more personal level.*
- *You cannot satisfy all groups but they all need your attention.*

4. Know Finance

In today's community college world a president must be innovative in developing new facilities, programs, and sources of revenue. Virtually every conversation about the current and future condition of community colleges laments the lack of resources. To function effectively in this environment, a leader must have a deeper knowledge of all aspects of finance for public institutions. Understanding all aspects of finance from budgets to bonds to investments is vital for all presidents. One president was so uncomfortable with her skill level in finance she decided to earn an MBA after her doctorate. Of course, a person needs to know how to lead strategic planning and execute that plan. Oftentimes, however, new leaders do not comprehend that equally important is prioritizing budget to match the goals of the strategic plan and get strategic buy-in when money is on the table.

No money, no mission.

5. Acquire Fundraising Abilities

Raising money is difficult. Learning how to cultivate fundraising through friendraising can make this process less daunting. Networking for revenue generation can be difficult. Fundraising entails asking for funds that support the educational mission. Realizing that fundraising is about the college and not the president makes asking less personal. Knowing that on any given day a person will not be embraced by everyone is just reality. Raising revenue requires learning how to get access to and work with all types of donors and funders. Learn about the different types of donations, gifts, and grants while keeping the focus on student success.

The fundraising goal is to help students be successful.

Part of the process is doing homework about the potential donor or philanthropic organization. Nothing is glamorous and there are no shortcuts to this tedious but essential preparation stage.

Develop a compelling ask for benefactors. Know your potential donor's passions and interests. Put the two together and you are ready.

Once a leader has the knowledge and a compelling case it is time to take the risk of "the ask" for the purpose of helping students be successful.

This job is not about running the college but about advocacy, fundraising, and community partnerships.

6. Learn to Navigate Politics and Advocate

Chancellors and presidents work with federal, state, and local elected officials. Advocacy is time consuming and requires learning how to maneuver politics.

I have a fear of politics and this can be intimidating. It takes training and practice.

Political navigation includes internal and external stakeholders in formal (testifying) and informal (ongoing relationships) advocacy. Knowing how to connect with legislators, no matter the political party, to carry out the mission of the community college is a learned skill. Being a president does open doors to learning how to leverage that role is advantageous. Crafting arguments for local advocacy, including stories of people who are part of their respective electorate, is important.

Learn how you connect with the legislature in order to convey the mission of community colleges. Like other aspects of leadership, you do not have to do this alone. Involve your board to be advocates for the college.

Knowledge of the laws of the state and staying current on legislative issues is the foundation for this work.

The reality is, politics trumps good sense.

7. Engage Faculty and Staff: Shared Governance

Several presidents noted the toughest challenges are not with the external stakeholders. The hardest trials are working with faculty on everything from quality of life to systemic change to workload issues. This was true for both union and nonunion colleges. A point to remember is that faculty at most community colleges have tenure or multiyear contracts. The faculty often remind presidents that they were at the college long before the president's arrival and will be at the college years after the president is gone. If a CEO desires to guide lasting systemic and strategic change, faculty must be engaged in driving the change.

No matter how mean faculty may be, they need my love.

At the heart of community colleges is the development of students. Colleges, however, must also invest in faculty because they are the people who pro-vide the services to help students lean and be successful in achieving their educational goals.

There are some faculty who do not understand "no" and throw tantrums. This may lead to a fight between myself and those faculty. I tell them if they disrespect me they will disrespect students. I care about faculty but I have to make deci-sions in the best interest of students.

As tough as it might be to work with different people throughout the college, presidents have little choice. All interviewees agreed that engaging college personnel in planning, decision making, and innovation is critical to suc-cess of the college. The job of the president is to fuel passion in others and surround oneself with smart people from throughout the college. Gen Xers talked of getting the right people in the room to address the issue at hand rather than standing committees due to the fast pace of change.

No pointing fingers. A president cannot throw anyone under the bus. Accept responsibility even if representing the collective will.

Success of students, faculty, staff, and the college is the pinnacle of trans-formational leadership. It is not about the president getting the credit. The thriving president knows true leadership is about accepting responsibility for mistakes and giving the acclaim for achievement to others.

8. Know Appropriate Use of Technology

Gen X presidents utilize technology extensively. They are always connected and multitasking is natural to them.

- *I admit I am married to my cell phone.*
- *I cannot turn it off. I am always thinking about the college. I go on vacation with my iPhone.*

They expect future presidents to employ technologies even more.

> *Today there is less need for presidents to travel. I never go to conferences unless I can take the kids. I do not go to conferences to connect and communicate with my presidential colleagues. I can do this through social media.*

They encourage leaders to be on twitter and social media. That being said, they implore future presidents to review their social media and public portfolio presence. While social media will not be part of the portfolio on the CV, hiring committees will review this when assessing a person for a leadership position.

Understanding how to evaluate the appropriate technology for faculty and students is important to the learning process. A president does not need to be an expert in technology but must have trustworthy staff to ascertain the cost/benefit of investment in technology. Technology is a major component of today's college infrastructure. From administrative functions to predictive analytics, technology is portrayed as the solution to efficiency and measurement. Overwhelmed with data and vendors, a leader needs to strategically plan how to utilize technology with laser focus on student success.

9. Develop Board Relations

A supportive board helps to accomplish the goals of the college. Future presidents need to understand that boards will not always be supportive. Learning the delicate dance of leading in tough times as well as amiable times is important. Not all board members will agree with every action or idea that is proposed by the president and leadership team. This is the norm and not the exception. Existing presidents need to be more transparent with future leaders about the realities of working with the five, seven, nine, or more individuals that come together to make up the governing board.

Educating the board is part of the president's work. Boards, whether elected or appointed, are political entities and can be valuable in advocacy.

Train the board to be effective advocates. Take them to ACCT conference and have them hang out with other board members.

The president has a vested interest and often viewed as the "hired gun" by external stakeholders. A board member is a volunteer serving in a governance position. The board member may have influence and sway politically due to being a kindred spirit with other political officials. The board member may also be a business leader in the community. Board members open doors for the president to talk with CEOs and others. Both of these facets of board relations are dependent upon the president and board member/s sharing the vision and commitment to student success for the benefit of the individual and the community.

(An observation by the authors: This topic of board relations made the top ten, but was discussed less among these presidents than in conversations with presidents of previous generations.)

10. Become Proficient in Identified Little Things

The last category includes a few little things that make a difference.

1. Negotiate the presidential contract, beyond the financial components, to reflect what is important to the individual's quality of life. Think about vacations, a future sabbatical, flexibility in schedules, and family concerns. Explore what is important to the local community. For example, is it customary for the president to entertain in his or her home? If so what needs to be included in the presidential contract to support this expectation? Or, is it customary to entertain at the local country club? If this is the case, should a membership be included as part of compensation? And what are the membership requirements of the county club and does that match with the president's and college's equity agenda?
2. Acquire impeccable manners. A president is constantly attending breakfast, lunch, and dinner meetings. It is paramount that the CEO knows proper dining etiquette.
3. Listen intently for warning signs that tough times are brewing. Tips and techniques for how to wear forty hats a day or drink from twenty-five fire hoses are needed tools in the leadership toolbox.
4. Develop a comfort level with people constantly asking, asking, and asking. Realizing a president cannot be all things to all people can help you stay in the presidential position longer.

5. Seize the opportunity of the first year. The first year of a presidency is around the clock. Learning the culture of the institution and developing relationships take time and there is a small window of opportunity to learn and develop. After the first year or so a president learns where to spend time and who and how to delegate with the leadership team.
6. Foster resilience. Gen Xers stressed that the presidency is a high-energy position that requires a tough skin and internal strength due to the high level of scrutiny and the demands of the many stakeholders.
   - *If your energy is low the job will eat you for lunch.*

CONCLUSION

Generation X presidents encourage ambitious, passionate, and talented individuals to acquire the skills and knowledge to become the future leaders of community college. They leave the reader with these questions.

- *What replenishes your soul and gives you energy?*
- *Why do you want to do this?*
- *Do you see the presidential position as fulfilling a mission in life? Do you want to bring faculty and staff together to help students?*

Seize the opportunity even if it does not coincide with your perceived professional timeline. Until someone is in the position there is little understanding of how it will change a life.

- *Finally, search your soul to see if you want to be a president.*
- *If you honestly want to be a president, then just do it.*
- *So, prepare well, take a leap of faith, and grow your wings on the way down.*

Bibliography

American Association of Community Colleges. 2012. *Reclaiming the American Dream Community Colleges and the Nation's Future*. Washington, DC: American Association of Community Colleges.

American Association of Community Colleges. 2013. AACC Competencies for Community College Leaders. *AACC Leadership Suite*.

Achieving the Dream, Inc. & The Aspen Institute. 2013. *Crisis and Opportunity: Aligning the Community College Presidency for Student Success*. June 21. Accessed on May 27, 2016. https://www.aspeninstitute.org/publications/crisis-opportunity-aligning-community-college-presidency-student-success/.

Ashford, Elle. 2016. "Gen-X Presidents Offer Different Perspective." *Community College Daily*. June 18. Accessed on June 18, 2016. http://www.ccdaily.com/Pages/Campus-Issues/Gen-X-presidents-offer-new-perspective-aspx.

Bailey, Thomas R., Shanna Smith Jaggars, and Davis Jenkins. 2015. *Redesigning America's Community Colleges: A Clearer Path to Student Success*. Cambridge, MA: Harvard University Press.

Boggs, George R. 2015. *Facing Change in the Community College: Leadership Issues and Challenges*. A joint publication of the Roueche Graduate Center, National American University and League for Innovation in the Community College.

Boggs, George R. and Christine J. McPhail. 2016. *Practical Leadership in Today's Community Colleges: Navigating Today's Challenges*. Hoboken, NJ: Jossey-Bass.

Carey, Kevin. 2015. *The End of College: Creating the Future of Learning and the University of Everywhere*. New York: Penquin.

Chopra, Rohit. 2013. *Student Debt Swells, Federal Loans Now Top a Trillion | Consumer Financial Protection Bureau.* July 17. Accessed on July 18, 2016. http://www.consumerfinance.gov/about-us/newsroom/student-debt-swells-federal-loans-now-top-a-trillion/.

Cook, Bryan J. 2012. "The American College President Study: Key Findings and Takeaways." *American Council on Education*. Accessed on January 21,

2016. http://www.acenet.edu/the-presidency/columns-and-features/Pages/The-American-College-President-Study.aspx.

Cooper, Susanna. 2016. "Tough Job If You Can Keep It." *Research Brief 1* (1). Wheelhouse: The Center for Community College Leadership and Research, University of California at Davis.

de los Santos, Gerardo and Mark Milliron. 2016. *2015 Trends*. Phoenix, AZ: League for Innovation.

Ellis, Martha M. 2012. "Preparing for Leadership Succession." In *Rising to the Challenge: Lessons Learned from Guilford Technical Community College*, edited by John E. Roueche and Suanne D. Roueche, 23-34. Washington, DC: Community College Press.

Fry, Richard. 2016. *Millennials Overtake Baby Boomers as America's Largest Generation. Pew Research Center*. April 26. Accessed on July 17, 2016. http://www.pewresearch.org/fact-tank/2016/04/25/millennials-overtake-baby-boomers/.

Kotter, John P. 2012. *Leading Change*. Cambridge, MA: Harvard Business Review Press.

Kram, Kathy E. and Lynn A. Isabella. "Mentoring Alternatives: The Role of Peer Relationships in Career Development." *Academy of Management Journal* 28:1 (1985): 110-133. Accessed on August 1, 2016. doi: 10.2307/256064.

Lancaster, Lynn C. and David Stillman. 2002. *When Generations Collide*. New York: Harper Business.

Lipka, Sara 2013, April 22. New chiefs of 2-year colleges must meet revenue and innovation challenges. *The Chronicle of Higher Education*. Retrieved from http://chronicle.com/article/New-College-Chiefs-Must-Meet/138727. Accessed May 23, 2016

McDade, Sharon A. "Teacher-Pupil: The Changing Relationships of Mentors and Protégé." *Community College Journal of Research and Practice* 29:9-10 (2005): 759-781. Accessed on August 1, 2016. doi: 10.1080/10668920591006629.

McLerran, Alice. 1995. *The Ghost Dance*. Toronto, Canada: Stoddard Publishing Co. Limited.

Murphy, Susan A. 2007. *Leading a Multigenerational Team*. AARP. Accessed on June 14, 2016. http://assets.aarp.org/www.aarp.org_/articles/money/employers/leading_multigenerational_workforce.pdf.

National Conference of State Legislators. 2015. *Performance-Based Funding for Higher Education*. July 31, 2015. Accessed on July 28, 2016. http://www.ncsl.org/research/education/performance-funding.aspx

Ort, Shirley. 2016. "Free college is a damaging myth." *Inside Higher Education*. July 19. Accessed on July 19, 2016. https://www.insidehighered.com/views/2016/07/19/free-or-no-loans-approach-will-undermine-access-college-essay.

Ostashevsky, Luba. 2016. "As Economy Rebounds, State Funding for Higher Education Isn't Bouncing Back." *The Hechinger Report*. September 14. Accessed on September 14, 2016. http://www.pbs.org/newshour/updates/economy-rebounds-state-funding-higher-education-isnt-bouncing-back/#.V9wuxAN69Uo.email.

Patterson, Constance. *Generation Stereotypes.* June. 36:6 (2005): Print version: 55. Accessed on June 13, 2016. http://www.apa.org/monitor/jun05/stereotypes.aspx.

Pew Research Center. 2010. *Millennials: A Portrait of Generation Next.* 2010. Accessed on August 16, 2016. http://www.pewsocialtrends.org/files/2010/10/millennials-confident-connected-open-to-change.pdf.

Phillippe, Kent A. 2016a. *AACC CEO Survey Compensation.* 2016. Accessed on July 17, 2016. http://www.aacc.nche.edu/Publications/Briefs/Documents/CEOSurvey_05012016.pdf.

Phillippe, Kent A. 2016b. "Diversity in Instructional Staff." *Data Points.* May. Accessed on July 17, 2016. http://www.aacc.nche.edu/Publications/datapoints/Documents/DP_Staff.pdf.

Phillippe, Kent A. 2016c. "Where the Revenue Comes from." *Data Points.* March. Accessed on July 17, 2016. http://www.aacc.nche.edu/Publications/datapoints/Documents/DP_CollegeRevenue.pdf.

Quinton, Sophie. 2016. *More States Start Funding Colleges Based on Outcomes. Stateline Pew Charitable Trust.* August 15. Accessed on August 15, 2016. http://www.pewtrusts.org/en/research-and-analysis/blogs/stateline/2016/08/15/more-states-start-funding-colleges-based-on-outcomes.

Rabey, Jeff. 2001. "The Role of Mentoring in Community College Presidential Preparation." PhD diss., Iowa State University.

Roueche, John E., George A. Baker III, and Robert R. Rose. 1989. *Shared Vision: Transformational Leadership in American Community Colleges.* Washington, DC: The Community College Press.

Shaffer, Joe. 2015. *Personal Interview with Ellis and Garcia.* May 28.

Selingo, Jeffrey J. 2016a. "The Job Nobody Can Seem to Keep: College President." *Washington Post,* July 15.

Selingo, Jeffrey J. 2016b. *Transformation Affecting Postsecondary Education.* White Paper. Charlottesville, VA: Miller Center University of Virginia.

Smith, Ashley A. 2016. "Tension at the Top." *Inside Higher Education.* May 20. https://www.insidehighered.com/news/2016/05/20/many-community-college-presidencies-are-upheaval. Accessed on June 7, 2016.

Staff Reporter. 2015. "Survey Reveals That Millennial Managers Are the New Face of American Business." *Workplace Trends.* Accessed on June 14, 2016. https://workplacetrends.com/the-multi-generational-leadership-study/.

Stark, Treca. 2015. "Leveraging Analytics in Community Colleges." *Educause Review.* September 14.

Strauss, William, and Neil Howe. 1991. *Generations: The History of America's Future, 1584-2069.* New York, NY: William Morrow and Company, Inc.

Strom, Stephen L., Alex A. Sanchez, and JoAnna Downey-Schilling. "Inside-Outside: Finding Future Community College Leaders." *The Community College Enterprise* 17:1 (2011): 9-21.

Suchman, Anthony L. and Gita Ramamurthy. 2014. "Physician Well-Being." In *Behavioral Medicine: A Guide for Clinical Practice,* 4th ed, edited by M. Feldman and J. Christensen, 51-56. China: McGraw Hill Education.

Taylor, Nicole F. 2014. *Tackling the Challenges of the Multigenerational Workforce.* Accessed on June 13, 2016. http://www.businessnewsdaily.com/6609-multigenerational-workforce-challenges.html#sthash.jvP61DdF.dpuf.

Teckle, Rahel. 2012. "Compensation and Benefits of Community College CEOs: 2012." *AACC Research Brief.* Accessed on June 14, 2016. http://www.aacc.nche.edu/AboutCC/Trends/Documents/CEOCompensationResearchBrief.pdf.

Texas Higher Education Coordinating Board. 2016. *2016 Texas Public Higher Education Almanac: A Profile of State and Institutional Performance and Characteristics.* Austin, TX: Texas Higher Education Coordinating Board.

Tugend, Alina. 2016. "A Meeting of Minds: Educators Discuss the Future of Higher Edcuation." *New York Times*, June 22: F4.

U.S. Department of Education, National Center for Education Statistics. 2016. *Fast Facts*. https://nces.ed.gov/fastfacts/display.aps?id=40. Accessed on July 30, 2016.

VanDerLinden, Kim E. "Learning to Play the Game: Professional Development and Mentoring." *Community College Journal of Research and Practice* 29:9-10 (2005): 729-743. Accessed on August 1, 2016. doi: 10.1080/10668920591006575.

Vaughan, George B. and Iris M. Weisman. 1998. *The Community College Presidency at the Millennium.* Washington, DC: American Association of Community Colleges.

Wazwaz, Noor. 2015 "It's Official: The U.S. is Becoming a Minority-Majority Nation." *U.S. News and World Report.* July 6. Accessed on July 25, 2016. http://www.usnews.com/news/articles/2015/07/06/its-official-the-us-is-becoming-a-minority-majority-nation.

Wyner, Joshua S. 2014. *What excellent community colleges do: Preparing all students for success.* Cambridge, MA: Harvard Education Press.

Zemke, Ron, Claire Raines, and Bob Filipcszk. 1999. *Generations at Work: Managing the Clash of Veterans, Boomers, Xers, and Nexters in Your Workplace.* New York: AMA Publications.

About the Editors

Martha M. Ellis, Ph.D., is vice president/dean of graduate faculty and professor in the Community College Leadership Program at the Roueche Graduate Center, National American University. She is also currently interim director of Higher Education Services at the Charles A. Dana Center, University of Texas at Austin. Martha is a leadership coach for Achieving the Dream. She recently served as interim president and CEO of the Texas Association of Community Colleges and facilitator for the High Performance Teams, Future Leaders Institute, and Presidents Academy Summer Institute for the American Association of Community Colleges.

Ellis previously was associate vice chancellor for Community College Partnerships at University of Texas System. She coordinated the UT System community college collaboratives between the fifty community college districts and universities as well as addressing statewide policy issues. She also chaired the executive committee for the UT distance education shared service alliance and the UT System Leadership Institute.

Martha has thirty-five years of experience in community colleges including two presidencies, provost, chief information officer, and faculty member. Ellis has won numerous teaching awards, has scholarly publications, and is an invited presenter at national conferences. Ellis was recognized by the Texas House of Representatives and US Congress for her leadership in community colleges.

Dr. Ellis is a member of the New York Academy of Sciences and the American Psychological Association. Ellis served on the Board of the American Association of Community Colleges, Commission on Colleges of SACSCOC, Board of Educational Affairs for the American Psychological Association, Commission on Women of the American Council on Education, and Executive Committee of Texas Association of Community Colleges.

She was president of the Association of Texas Colleges and Universities. In addition to her Ph.D. from the University of North Texas, she completed postgraduate work at Columbia University in New York, an internship at the Albert Ellis Institute at State University of New York, and the President's Institute at Harvard University.

Linda L. García, Ph.D., is assistant director of College Relations for the Center for Community College Student Engagement, part of the Program in Higher Education Leadership at The University of Texas at Austin. She oversees the Center's community college relations and serves as a point of contact for state leaders, funders, and national higher education organizations.

Linda previously served as the vice president of Community College Relations at National American University. She has also worked at Lone Star College, Maricopa Community Colleges and The University of Texas at Brownsville and Texas Southmost College. Linda's experience includes student development, instructional support, and teaching.

Linda earned a degree in Bachelor of Journalism with a concentration in broadcast and a Doctorate in higher education administration with a specialization in community college leadership from The University of Texas at Austin. Her Master of Arts in Interdisciplinary Studies degree is from The University of Texas at Brownsville. Linda also serves on the board of the National Council on Student Development, an affiliate council of the American Association of Community Colleges.

About the Contributors

JoAlice Blondin, Ph.D., became the fifth president of Clark State Community College on July 1, 2013. Prior to Clark State, Dr. Blondin served as chancellor of Arkansas Tech University–Ozark Campus and professor of English for seven years, as well as chief academic officer, chief student officer, department chair of English, Communication, and Social Sciences and instructor of English. She holds a Ph.D. in English from Arizona State University; Master of Arts in English from Arizona State University; and Bachelor of Arts from Purdue University majoring in English with a minor in Spanish.

Dr. Blondin focuses all of her efforts on realizing the mission of the institutions she serves and is known for both her student-centered approach and her emphasis on regional economic development. She serves on the boards of the Dayton Development Coalition, Springfield Chamber of Commerce, Community Mercy Hospital Foundation, and Opportunities for Individual Change, and is vice chair of the Southwestern Ohio Council for Higher Education and president-elect of the National Council for Workforce Education. She serves on the Ohio Association of Community Colleges' Student Success Council, and is a member of the Springfield Rotary Club. Dr. Blondin lives in Springfield with her husband, Andy Fox, who is a systems analyst for ABF Freight Systems. Their daughter, Helena, is a senior at The Ohio State University studying biology and animal science.

Thom D. Chesney, Ph.D., has been president of Brookhaven College since August 2011. For three years prior he served as associate provost for student success and assessment, associate professor of arts and humanities, and accreditation liaison for The University of Texas at Dallas. While at UT Dallas, he initiated the university's GEMS (Gateways to Excellence in

Math and Science) quality enhancement plan, which helped effect dramatic improvements in undergraduate student performance in science, technology, engineering, and mathematics courses. From 2004 to 2008, Thom served as district vice president of academic affairs and provost of Collin College (TX), having joined the college as district dean of communications and humanities in 2003. He previously held administrative and faculty positions in Pennsylvania and Washington. He earned his doctorate in English literature from Florida State University, a Master of Arts degree in creative writing from Minnesota State University, Mankato; and a Bachelor of Arts degree in Spanish with a minor in business administration from Washington University in St Louis.

In addition to his portfolio of academic experience, Thom serves on the American Association of Community College's (AACC) Commission on Economic and Workforce Development; the American Council on Education (ACE) Spectrum Advancing Leadership Program, and boards of the North Texas Community College Consortium and Metrocrest Chamber of Commerce; is currently in his eighth year as chair of the leadership programs advisory committee for the McKinney Chamber of Commerce; served for four years on the city of McKinney Arts Commission (one as chair); has been recognized as 2014 Metrocrest Citizen of the Year and one of Collin County's twenty-one leaders for the twenty-first century; and has over the years offered his voice and writing talents to Minnesota and Florida Public Radio, live theater, and a variety of other print and broadcast media. A Washington University Bear some thirty years ago and a Brookhaven College Bear today, Thom has always been a passionate participant in and fan of intercollegiate athletics, as well.

Allen Goben, Ed.D., is president at Tarrant County College District's Northeast Campus near Ft. Worth, TX and in his tenth year at the presidential level. Prior presidential work included service at Heartland Community College in Illinois and president of Hazard Community and Technical College (HCTC) in Kentucky. Allen was named to the twenty-first-century commission on the Future of Community Colleges in 2011 by the American Association of Community Colleges, complementing his service on AACC's Voluntary Framework of Accountability Steering Committee. In 2009, he was honored as a Distinguished Graduate at The University of Texas at Austin in community college leadership, and he now teaches doctoral students in similar programs at National American University and Ferris State. Allen's classroom teaching experience includes history, geography, social studies, communications, human relations, and doctoral level college leadership, and he has worked as a counselor at both the high school and college level.

A first-generation college student who began studies at Indian Hills Community College in Iowa, Allen completed a bachelor's degree in History from Iowa State University, a master's degree in School Counseling from Drake University, and a doctoral degree in Educational Administration from The University of Texas at Austin, Community College Leadership Program. Allen and his wife Kelly enjoy life with three amazing daughters: Natalie, Riley, and Halley.

Steven R. Gonzales, Ed.D., has served as the president of GateWay Community College since July 2013. Dr. Gonzales has more than eighteen years of instructional and administrative experience in higher education. From 1998 to 2013, he served in several progressive roles, acting associate vice president of academic affairs and chief academic officer, dean of communications, math, and learning support, associate dean of academic services, mathematics professor, and developmental education specialist in mathematics, for the Pinal County Community College District that operates as Central Arizona College. Steven is actively engaged in national organizations such as American Association of Community Colleges Board of Directors and National Community College Hispanic Council, National Association for Community College Entrepreneurship, and Hispanic Association of Colleges and Universities. He is actively involved in the Phoenix community. Dr. Gonzales is an adjunct faculty member of the Mary Lou Foulton Teachers College at Arizona State University and the Roueche Graduate Center's Community College Leadership Program for National American University.

Dr. Gonzales earned his doctorate in educational administration from Community College Leadership Program from the University of Texas at Austin. He was awarded a University Preemptive Fellowship, as well as the John and Suanne Roueche Fellowship. He holds a Master of Arts in teaching mathematics and Bachelor of Science in secondary education—mathematics from Northern Arizona University. Dr. Gonzales has a large blended family with five children ranging in ages from four to seventeen. Away from work, he enjoys outdoor activities such as hunting, fishing, and golfing.

Stefani Gray Hicswa, Ph.D., assumed Northwest College's presidency July 15, 2013 in Wyoming. Prior to her arrival, Dr. Hicswa served seven years as president of Miles Community College in Montana, where she helped increase graduation rates to first among all postsecondary institutions in Montana and among the top community colleges in the nation. She previously operated a consulting firm in Wilsall, Montana, that specialized in strategic planning and organizational development. Hicswa was named to the Higher Education Research and Development Institute nationwide advisory board; serves as a visiting professor for National American University's doctoral program in

Community College Leadership; and presenter at the American Association for Women in Community Colleges CEO retreat in Maryland.

President Hicswa holds a doctorate in educational administration from the University of Texas at Austin. She was honored in 2007 as a Distinguished Graduate at The University of Texas at Austin in recognition of her work in community college leadership. She earned her master's in adult, community, and higher education from Montana State University in Bozeman and a bachelor's in organizational communication from the University of Montana in Missoula. Raised in Dillon, Montana, Stefani is married to Scott Hicswa, a consulting forester. They have two sons, Kalin and Keegan.

Kirk A. Nooks, Ed.D., became president of the Longview campus of Metropolitan Community College Kansas City in 2013. Previously Nooks was a campus dean and executive liaison for diversity at Georgia Highlands College. An engineer by training, Kirk has fifteen years of experience in education, business, and engineering. Nooks holds a doctorate in higher education administration from The George Washington University, an MBA in marketing and a bachelor of science in industrial management from Mercer University. He is a graduate of the Thomas Lakin Institute for Mentored Leadership and a member of the inaugural cohort of the American Council on Education's Spectrum Leadership Institute.

Nooks is involved with the Lee's Summit Chamber of Commerce and the Missouri Community College Association. Nooks has also been involved with the Association for the Study of Higher Education, The Chair Academy, National Academic Advising Association, the National Association of College & University Business Officers, the National Association for Student Personnel Administrators, the National Council on Black American Affairs and the National Council on Student Development, the American Association of Community Colleges, and the Association of American Colleges and Universities.

Kathleen Plinske, Ed.D., serves as campus president of the Osceola, Lake Nona, and Poinciana Campuses at Valencia College in Orlando, Florida. Before joining Valencia in 2010, Plinske began her career at McHenry County College, a community college in her hometown of Crystal Lake, Illinois. She was hired as an instructional media specialist in 2001, and moved into a number of different roles over the next nine years, including vice president of Institutional Effectiveness, and ultimately, interim president. She has also served as a part-time faculty member at McHenry County College, Valencia College, the University of Central Florida, and Pepperdine University. Actively involved in her community, Plinske has served as board chair of the Education Foundation of Osceola County and as president of the

Rotary Club of Lake Nona. She has also served on the Board of CareerSource Central Florida, the Osceola Center for the Arts, Junior Achievement of Osceola County, and the Lake Nona Education Council.

A graduate of the Illinois Mathematics and Science Academy, Plinske attended Indiana University-Bloomington as a Herman B. Wells Scholar, earning a Bachelor of Arts in Spanish and Physics with highest distinction and honors. A member of Phi Beta Kappa, she completed a Master of Arts in Spanish from Roosevelt University, a Doctorate in Educational Technology from Pepperdine University, and a Master of Business Administration from the University of Florida. In 2010, Plinske was recognized as one of twenty-four emerging leaders in the world by Phi Delta Kappa. She was named 2012 Woman of the Year by the Orlando Business Journal in its 40 Under 40 competition and the 2012 Outstanding Young Alumnus by Indiana University. She received the 2013 Alumni Distinguished Leadership Award from the Illinois Mathematics and Science Academy, and in 2014 received the Compadre Award from the Hispanic Business Council of the Kissimmee/Osceola Chamber of Commerce and the Don Quijote Hispanic Community Champion Award from the Hispanic Chamber of Commerce of Metro Orlando. Plinske was selected as an Aspen Presidential Fellow in 2016. Plinske is happily married to her husband, Larry W. Tyree, who shares her love for golf, the Chicago Cubs, and their dog, Cooper.